Build and Manage Your Music Career

by Maurice Johnson

Edited by Carolyn Engelmann

236 Georgia Street, Suite 100
Vallejo, CA 94608

Library of Congress Catalog Card Number: 99-62537

Cover Design: Linda Gough
Book Design and Layout: Linda Gough
Production Staff: Mike Lawson, publisher; Carolyn Engelmann, editor

MixBooks is an imprint of artistpro.com, LLC
236 Georgia Street, Suite 100
Vallejo, CA 94590
707-554-1935

Also from MixBooks
The AudioPro Home Recording Course, Volumes I, II, and III
I Hate the Man Who Runs This Bar!
The Mastering Engineer's Handbook
Making Music with Your Computer, 2nd Ed.
How to Make Money Scoring Soundtracks and Jingles
The Art of Mixing: A Visual Guide to Recording, Engineering, and Production
500 Songwriting Ideas (For Brave and Passionate People)
Music Publishing: The Real Road to Music Business Success, Rev. and Exp. 5th Ed.
How to Run a Recording Session
Mix Reference Disc, Deluxe Ed.
The Songwriters Guide to Collaboration, Rev. and Exp. 2nd Ed.
Critical Listening and Auditory Perception
Modular Digital Multitracks: The Power User's Guide, Rev. Ed.
The Dictionary of Music Business Terms
Professional Microphone Techniques
Sound for Picture, 2nd Ed.
Music Producers, 2nd Ed.
Live Sound Reinforcement

Also from EMBooks
The Independent Working Musician
Making the Ultimate Demo, 2nd Ed.
Anatomy of a Home Studio
The EM Guide to the Roland VS-880

Second Printing
Printed in Auburn Hills, MI
ISBN 0-87288-725-1

Who This Book Is For...

If you ever feel unsure or unconfident
when it comes to booking gigs...

If you have ever felt uneasy when asked to
state your price to a potential client...

If your fear of failure is greater than your desire
to succeed as a working musician...

If you are interested in starting a band or
performing solo but have never set foot on a stage
or don't have any idea how to get started...

If you would like to learn to run your band
like the business that it is...

If you want to sharpen your knowledge about
working as an independent musician/entrepreneur...

If you need a real understanding of the
rudimentary aspects of booking, self-promotion
or self-management...

If you or your band seem disorganized,
show a lack of basic business smarts,
and have no sense of direction...

If anyone has ever said you don't know the
first thing about starting or performing in a band...

If your parents tell you that you'll never
amount to anything working as a musician...

If you would like to become more than average
among your musician peers...

...this book is for you.

To my mother for empowering me with the gift of tenacity.

To my brother David for introducing me to the world of music.

To my wife and my children, Rita, Nachole, and Timmy,
for tolerating my rambling on morning, noon and night.

And to musician friends, acquaintances, and others for whom this book was written;
had it not been for your questions, this book would not exist.

Thanks, everyone!

Contents

Foreword

Knowledge is power! And if it's true that all the great knowledge in the world is contained in books, then this book is a great place to start to empower yourself. Back when I was a teenage recording artist in the late '70s, it was uncool to be a musician and think of it as a business. Now, it is common knowledge that if you just play dumb and leave your business matters to the "suits," you will just get nowhere—and have nothing when you get there.

Maurice Johnson has done a great job of laying it all out step-by-step for you in this book. As you read it you will learn all about this exciting music business world so that you are prepared to do what needs to be done to get where you need to go. This book can help you make all your dreams come true.

WALLACE COLLINS

Wallace Collins is an entertainment and intellectual-property lawyer in New York who represents prominent recording artists, producers, and managers. He was a recording artist for Epic records before attending Fordham Law School.

Introduction

A STATEMENT OF EMPOWERMENT

You only need to hear this once: *"You can build and manage your own music career!"* I say this because it is a statement of empowerment.

Time and time again many individuals never get around to challenging their own personal potential. Sometimes all it takes is for someone else to say, "You can do that!" and then something clicks and you're on your way.

I remember something my mother told me more than 30 years ago. Not quite five years old at the time, I had just run into the living room after playing in the dirt or something. She was just standing there, as if expecting me, with this blank look on her face, and she said to me, "Son, God has a gift for you." A few months later she had a stroke and died. Those words have never left my memory. In a way, that was her statement of empowerment to me.

Always in search of the gift my mother spoke of, I challenged myself and pursued almost every opportunity that came my way, including this book. To this day the search continues.

With everything, you will find a road to travel and it won't always be easy. Bear in mind that things that come too easily are often short-lived. This book is a mere reflection of one road that I have traveled. All I have done is kicked aside a few stones and laid down some markers. The rest is up to you…. *You can do this!*

BEFORE WE BEGIN

After some consideration and much thought on the topic of effectively managing one's own music career, the question remains, aren't there already enough books on this subject? Apparently not. I've compiled this work in an effort to abolish the absence of at least one more resource for the knowledge-hungry musician.

The truth is, a curious number of questions are posed to me by young musicians, as well as by a surprising number of experienced players. While a book like *This Business of Music* (Krasilovsky and Shemel, 1995), crowned as the bible of the industry, reveals more of the inner workings of the music industry itself, its sheer depth can overwhelm or even intimidate an unsuspecting newcomer.

My objective is to offer insight and practical solutions to common questions and scenarios shared by many working and aspiring musicians in a user-friendly, yet challenging, forum. Here is a wide assortment of useful information that I strongly advise you and other musicians like you to take full advantage of and share with others along the way.

A CLOSER LOOK AT THE LOCAL MUSIC SCENE

Go among the local musicians just about anywhere on the planet, and virtually every one will report a seemingly diminishing appreciation for their civic contributions by the general public. My application of the term *local* refers to the geographic location in which one resides and performs on a regular or more permanent basis. Observation and fact reveal that the self-esteem of many hard-working local musicians is in dire straits. Many corporate-owned clubs, hotels, and restaurants, by way of downsizing and budget cuts, can't justify live music as a valid expense and consequently force musicians to assume a subordinate role. The local musician who has dreams beyond his or her general domain is often met with discouragement as smaller, independently owned clubs adopt the notion, "Why should I book a local band for *x* amount of money?" and then hire an out-of-town band for a guaranteed base plus a percentage of the door. The resulting effect could make for a less pleasing conclusion as the local springboard stiffens to a rigid and unsuitable launching pad for fledgling bands and musicians.

THERE IS A BRIGHT SIDE

View this book as the thread to weave your own silver lining. You may not grasp the full scope in the first reading, so take small portions of the information, allowing yourself ample time to digest new concepts and unfamiliar terms. Refer to this book over and over as the need arises, just as you would with any other reference source. I also encourage you to share this information with other musicians so that it may exemplify and perpetuate the theory that knowledge is power.

AUTHOR'S DISCLAIMER

This book is designed to be a general guide to educate musicians and other performing artists on basic booking and self-promotion techniques. The information included is based on personal experience in booking and self-promotion. I make no claims to be an authority on these subjects and am not engaged in rendering legal or professional advice. I claim no liability or responsibility to anyone with respect to contracts, negotiations, or agreements that may result from information in this book, or for any loss or damage caused by or alleged to have been caused directly or indirectly by this information.

A FEW DEFINITIONS

Throughout this book I refer to the terms *key person, prospect,* and *client.* Below are the definitions as I apply them.

Key Person

Often called the contact person, this is the primary individual of authority with whom you will work closely during negotiation and other business matters regarding the employment and maintenance of your services.

Prospect

A potential client with whom you have not previously done business. In this case, a person who may want to hire you or your band.

Client

A person with whom you are currently doing business; that is, someone who has signed a contract and paid a deposit.

Answer the following questions as best you can.

If anything were possible, what would you like to achieve as a musician?

_____

_____

_____

_____

_____

_____

_____

_____

_____

Can you list five things you could do to make this happen?

1 _____

2. _____

3. _____

4. _____

5. _____

You, the Musician

T he early years of your music career will be guided mostly by trial and error—and believe me, if you're not careful, error will do most of the driving. But let's face it, that's how most musicians get their start.

Now, we're going to back up and begin with some important basics. Let's start with a personal overview or self-evaluation. Take a few minutes to mentally review the following list of questions and then draw your own silent but truthful conclusions.

- What are your salable qualities or attributes as a musician/performing artist?

- Do you have the self-discipline to employ organizational tools such as daily, weekly, or monthly planners; schedules; earning and expense tracking software; etc.?

- When faced with competition or tough situations, how would you rate your tolerance level on a scale of one to ten?

You are responsible for your own first steps; no one can make them for you. You must start by deciding what your ultimate goals are, and then put yourself in charge. Make your own decisions and view yourself truthfully and realistically. Don't set unrealistic goals, and by all means, don't procrastinate. Be careful not to use any of these as an excuse for failure.

A LESSON IN APPRECIATION

As a young boy growing up in a small Oklahoma town, I recall, I spent many evenings with a great guitarist friend, Mr. Larry Carol Puckett. I was often amused and amazed watching him, seated in his lazy-boy chair, playing his guitar with the Lawrence Welk orchestra accompanying him via his television set. For Carol, this was a typical form of entertainment. It was funny how he'd sit there playing every song throughout the entire show—

"Polka Dots and Moonbeams," "Stella by Starlight," "Tie a Yellow Ribbon 'Round the Old Oak Tree." There wasn't a song that he didn't know. Being an impressionable 16-year-old at the time, I was fascinated.

I was recently reunited with my friend after more than twenty years, now in his 70s and a little less steady of hand. I was inspired to include this brief synopsis of our relationship out of sheer respect and appreciation for having known and learned from such a terrific individual.

There is knowledge to be learned from everyone. Don't shut out any sources that can gain you useful and important knowledge. Education doesn't always come from books. It's the practical training and experience through real-life interaction and personal investigation that will reap you the greatest benefits in the long run. Thanks Carol!

THE CLOSET MUSICIAN

I've met some great musicians, and some not-so-great, who all shared a common desire to play with a band or start their own. Another commonality among them was that they never ventured outside their homes much, which brings me to another important point: coming out of the closet as a musician. The closet musician with a desire to finally set foot on stage may initially feel awkward or lack the slightest idea of how to get started. I'll assume you have a pretty good idea of who the local bands are in your area and where some of them play. Armed with this information, begin by setting aside at least two hours each weekend to visit some of the spots where local bands are playing. Generally, these will be club or restaurant settings.

I am aware that some of you don't take too kindly to clubs, but let's face it, this is where you'll find most working musicians. If this is an issue of concern, view it from the perspective that a good musician will always appreciate the support of other musicians, and *you* might very well be the support they're in need of. Getting started doesn't just happen by accident—you have to put forth a good deal of effort. Your second step is to build a network of musicians who are working regularly and make it a point to become a familiar face in each of their audiences. Make them aware that you are a musician, too, with an interest in performing in the local music scene.

The musician as an audience member brings new meaning to the term *audience participation*. Be prepared, and seize every opportunity to sit in with a band. Whether it's for one song or an entire set, this is one of the most important moves toward eventually stepping out on your own. Clubs with house bands that play on a regular basis often promote jam sessions or open-mic nights.

INGREDIENTS FOR SUCCESS

Have you ever thrown a stone into a pond and watched the ripples it creates? As the stone breaks the surface of the water, the entire pond is affected. Now, visualize that stone as yourself and all your efforts. The greater the effort, the larger the stone. If you can envision your efforts as ripples, you can begin to get a good understanding of how you can affect the scope of your own success. Some people excel faster than others only because of various circumstantial factors. It may be a matter of economics, geographic location, resourcefulness, or sheer determination. In truth, we all start out with the same success potential.

Ambition and Self-Belief

Like the law of motion, ambition can be defined as *the law of motivation*—that perpetual spirit that fuels the hearts of many of the world's musical geniuses and those yet to come.

Another key ingredient to your success as a working musician is to first believe in yourself. Your self-belief can outweigh occasions when things don't appear to be moving in an upward direction. Over time, you will find that other musicians won't have the same goals you do. In fact, most individuals who either pick up an instrument or study some form of music will abandon their initial desire to become a professional musician at the first sign of adversity or discontent. A good friend of mine made a excellent observation when he pointed out that what separates the average working musician from the more successful musicians in the industry is a simple principle known as *cause and effect*. By this he meant that the more energy you put into something, the greater the final outcome or end result will be.

Persistence

Persistence is the next ingredient we'll heave into our cauldron of success. You'll never know unless you try; and if you fail, try again. That's really the definition of persistence, in a nutshell. Persistence has allowed humans to achieve the power of flight and explore the outermost regions of space. No matter how monumental a task appears to be, persistence will eventually offer gratifying rewards. At times, others will recognize your persistence and react in your favor because of it. Try to remember back when you played your first chord or performed for the first time in public without having the jitters. It was your persistence that saw you through each moment of your own evolution. That same persistence will see you through greater achievements yet to come. In the academic world, students are classified in two categories, *achievers* and *nonachievers*. Here again, people progress at different rates. For the so-called nonachiever, their lack of persistence becomes the primary dividing factor.

Sharing Your Knowledge

Every achievement and every experience is valuable. From this moment on, I want you to make it a point to pass on what you have learned to other musicians. To this day, musicians stop me and ask questions regarding the music business, and before long, I find myself reeling through my own personal library of experiences to find the answers. I can't help remembering that I was once a young musician with some of the same questions and no choice but to find my own answers through trial and error.

Expanding Your Music Opportunities

Learn new things. Think of the many different ways you can apply your musical skills. You may want to consider giving private lessons or working in a music store for starters. Playing in a band can be tough during lean times when your band is not so busy. Keep your mind open to new ideas. You can really cripple yourself when you close your mind to opportunities. Look into the possibility of working with other bands as a sideman. Talk to other musicians who are using their musical skills in different ways. Do you have recording equipment? Offer your studio services to small bands or songwriters to record demos. Contact local ad agencies and television and radio stations to contract as a jingle writer.

A Basic Sense of Organization

For a basic tool, I suggest my first book, *The New! Working Musician's One Year Organizer*. In it, you'll find a one-year planning calendar that lets you start at any month of the year and includes general expense tracking for each month and a musician's monthly payroll. I've included three databases: Musicians' Contacts and Stand-ins; Clubs and Restaurants; and Leads and Follow-Ups. The book also includes a contract for you to use and lots of other important tools you'll need to organize your band. It was written for you. Make sure that every member of your band gets one each year. Ask your local bookstore to look up this ISBN number: 0-7866-1822-1.

SUGGESTIONS TO HELP YOU GET ORGANIZED

- Purchase a monthly planner.

- For computer users, employ software that will help you manage your music career. (To obtain such a program, type in www.giglogic.com the next time you're online and download a copy of *Gig-O-Rama*.)

- Secure a stable post office box for professional correspondence, such as royalties and contracts. Never use an apartment address for your professional business correspondence. Many musicians lose or never receive important documents sent to them by mail because street addresses are unstable due to relocation, divorce or separation, and so on. Usually a post office box can be rented for as little as $50 a year. After you have secured a post office box, have all stationery, envelopes, and business cards printed with your P.O. box number.

- Print your contract in duplicate on NCR (no carbon required) forms. Keep an ample supply on hand at all times.

- To expedite client correspondence, e.g., returning a signed contract, obtain a rubber stamp with your name or your band's name and address.

- Always keep plenty of business cards on hand. Don't wait until you run completely out before reordering.

- Find a printer who is both reasonable and trustworthy. Over time your printer will become familiar with your needs and be willing to fill your order more cost-effectively than other printers. A good relationship between you and your printer can ensure special care and attention to your print job.

- Obtain a briefcase and let it serve as a miniature version of your home office. Inside it you should include basic business items: press kits, demo tapes, postcards, business cards, envelopes, contracts, your organizer, a legal pad, stamps, pens, pencils, paper clips, resumes, etc. Of course, only a few of these items will be necessary to prepare you for each given business situation. Get accustomed to carrying a briefcase regularly. If you're ever approached by a serious prospect who is ready to do business and find yourself unprepared without a briefcase, you will understand its importance.

Dress for Success

First impression is everything. We can all relate to the sense of self-confidence a new suit of clothes can give us. It's funny how a particular style of clothing or personal adornment can convey a particular attitude. For instance, take a look at the so-called "generation X." Today's youth use bizarre body piercing and alarming haircuts to express their individuality. In this desire for self-expression, they are not unlike every generation before them.

Nonetheless, try to remember and apply this simple rule of thumb: the first impression is the most lasting impression. Whether we realize it or not, people watch and observe each other every day. We are not only being peered at and picked apart on a daily basis—worse, we're being judged. So dress thoughtfully and accordingly as you conduct preliminary business. When it's time to perform, *then* it's time to portray the stage image your band represents.

Check It Out! ▶ *If you're in school, stay and finish. Knowledge is truly the most powerful tool that anyone can possess. It's up to you to seek it out and use it wisely. It's good to have a dream, but it is also good to know that you can earn a living because you stuck it out and pursued your education.*

No clearly means *no,* and we've been taught, conditioned, and continuously reminded of its profound and unwavering meaning since we were toddlers. Maybe that's why the word is so feared by most individuals. Just look at the risks that I have to take. Perhaps you're reading this at your local library or in a bookstore. When it comes time to check it out or buy it, you might say "No! What do I need this for?" That's a chance my publisher and I have to take. It's as simple as that.

The next time you think, *"What if they say no?"* stop and ask yourself, *"But what if they say yes?"* At some point in your music career you will need to prepare yourself for the times when you'll hear the response, "No," and know how to act upon it. The fear of rejection is a common one that all of us have felt at one time or another. When it comes to booking gigs, you must be confident and persistent. "No" is a temporary barrier—you only have to figure out how to get around it.

Eight Ways to Combat Rejection Before It Happens

- Don't view rejection as a final conclusion.

- Always establish at least three options before you submit an idea or make a proposal. For example, if you're trying to convince a restaurant owner to hire you in an establishment that doesn't normally have live music, you could offer to (1) play as a scaled-down combo for a smaller fee; (2) play short sets; or (3) work on a week-by-week, trial basis so they don't have to make a long-term commitment right away.

- Ask the individual who rejected your proposal for suggestions, and if they would re-evaluate your proposal after you have employed their suggestions.

- Use third-party influence (that is, mention someone the prospect knows) to walk your idea in—for example, "Mr. Edwards suggested that I speak with you."

- Look at your idea from as many angles as possible. Is there another market or direction you could pursue?

- Find out as much as you can about a prospect before presenting your proposal or idea.

- Learn from rejections and refusals and apply what you have learned before making your next proposal.

- List as many reasons as you can why a prospect might accept your proposal, then list reasons why they might refuse your proposal. Giving yourself a complete picture of the possible outcomes will allow you to build the most effective strategy before you approach the prospect. In the end, the decision may rest on factors beyond your control, such as a non-negotiable budget; knowing why you may get a negative response will help you avoid taking it personally.

YOUR EMOTIONAL SUPPORT FACTORS

The musician/performing artist who relies solely on his or her craft as a primary means of income may sometimes find it extra difficult and trying. Emotional support outside of your own ambition and determination is essential to the progress and success rate of any career. Lack of emotional support from a spouse or significant other can create unnecessary grief and hardship, which, history has shown, can even lead to separation or divorce in some cases.

There are a number of reasons why spouses and significant others sometimes have difficulty showing support for their performing-artist mates. They may perceive your tenacious efforts and determination as selfish or feel that you've turned your back on family obligations as you pursue an unrealistic dream. Perhaps the problem is envy—they may consider them-selves nonachievers and may truly wish they had your drive, nerve, and determination to pursue a dream.

If your partner has a strongly realistic nature, he or she may have difficulty understanding your reasoning. A realist deals only with factual information weighed against potential outcome, e.g., gainful employment equals a specific number of hours at a specific hourly wage, equaling a total of *x* dollars. Repeat that process five days per week multiplied by 52 weeks in a year and *presto!* you're making a living.

One way to build emotional support factors is to include your spouse or significant other in the action. Rather than taking the bull by the horns all by yourself, why not ask your partner to help? Often a significant other will feel left out because she just doesn't know what to do. No one knows what you're thinking or what your method of operation is unless you tell them. You can make your partner feel helpful simply by putting her in charge of a mailing list or assembling and sending out press kits. Better yet, let her choose how she would like to assist you. Put this idea into action by changing the way you approach things. That task you set out to do on your own, make it a two-person job. Let your partner feel as if she, too, has a hand in the success of your career.

COPING WITH NEGATIVE INPUT

Another recognized factor among many musicians is negative input from peers. If taken too seriously, this can eat away at your self-confidence. The best way to deal with negative input is not to deal with it at all. True, constructive criticism is critical to the development of anyone with an aspiring, goal-oriented nature. There's no harm in a critical analysis when the critic's intentions are well-meaning and not derisive. In developing your skill and sense of professional judgment, you can benefit from the vantage point of an outsider: often a relative, spouse, or close friend will notice things that you may have overlooked and offer helpful suggestions or advice.

As you become more accustomed and tuned to your craft, make a concerted effort not to dwell on the opinions of others. Graduate yourself to the next level of professionalism: self-empowerment. Empower yourself with your own reassurance and self-confidence. Don't listen to everybody because everyone has an opinion (and you know what they say about opinions). Beyond a certain point, constructive criticism can become destructive if you let it. Whatever you do, don't focus on criticism or lose sleep over it. By allowing the opinions of others to disturb your train of thought, you open the door and invite everyone else to join in and chisel away at your confidence whenever the feeling hits them.

 *You must become focused and comfortable with who you are without comparing yourself to anyone else. View negative energy as poison, and have nothing to do with it!*

LOSING THE AMATEUR MIND-SET

If your goal truly is to become a working musician, you must lose the amateur mind-set. Recognize that you're in it for higher stakes. As you move among the ranks of your working-musician peers, there will be times when those who are unconfident or envious will zealously challenge your competence as a professional. You have what it takes be a professional, and you must never let anyone tell you otherwise. There are many musicians out there looking for approval and acceptance while basing their success on some individual's opinion. We see examples of this with things like talent shows. Talent shows have the elusive potential of being a launching pad that leads to greater things. But remember, talent shows are for amateurs! I suppose a person could become a "professional" talent-show participant, given enough opportunities, but in the real world—away from competitors, runners up, and the "panels of experts,"—there are no grand prize winners. While it is true that some of the world-recognized talent shows have debuted many of today's up-and-coming singers and musical groups, the talent-show scene can often cause some to fall short and lose sight of their real goals as they pursue a not-so-grand prize.

If you're considering participating in talent shows, remember these three things: (1) know when to draw the line; (2) don't make a career of it; and (3) don't stay in the talent-show circuit too long, or you may harm your professional reputation.

A Few Suggestions to Help You Think Like a Professional

Although it's common for early-career musicians and fledgling bands to feel a little less competent and creditable than their more established peers, it is important to think and act like a professional at all times.

- Don't compare yourself to more accomplished musicians or performers. Such comparisons are unfair to you and never allow you to grow and evolve individually.

- Try not to think competitively.

- Show respect to fellow musicians but avoid subordinating yourself to them. For instance, don't pester them excessively for advice, or you might brand yourself with the status of student or amateur.

- During a live performance, never stop a song in the middle. Keep track in your head and resume playing when you reach a familiar section. Stopping a song shows unfamiliarity with the material or lack of confidence and is the mark of a rank amateur. An inexperienced musician might adopt this bad habit if he's not careful. Be aware, if this describes you, and make a concentrated effort to arrest the habit.

- Avoid the notion "I'm not ready yet."

- Assume that your talents are worth someone's money.

- Adopt the idea that you can learn something from everyone, no matter what level they're on.

- Never think that you know all there is to know about being a good performer.

- Don't be selfish—always be willing to share *your* knowledge with anyone who has an earnest desire to learn.

GO AHEAD AND JAM!

You can discover a whole new sense of satisfaction and keep your chops up at the same time. Whether or not you're regularly with a band, it's important to occasionally attend jam sessions. While a jam session is not a paying gig, there are a lot of benefits and rewards that can come from this simple activity as you develop your own social and performance skills.

Here Are a Few Ways Jam Sessions Can Benefit You

- They're an excellent way to keep your chops up between gigs.

- They put you in the company of other musicians, which could generate additional performance opportunities.

- They are the perfect way to network with the general public, as well as other musicians.

- They give you the opportunity to develop your stage presence.

- They expose you to an audience that may not frequent the clubs or other establishments where you normally perform.

- Whereas at a paying gig you perform to please an audience, a jam session is an outlet for musicians to entertain themselves for the sheer fun and satisfaction of it.

A DIP IN THE COMPETITIVE POOL

In case you haven't noticed, I don't condone having a competitive or adversarial spirit. Look at other musicians as allies, not opponents. Yes, the music industry may often be driven by a strong competitive influence. But for you, competitive thinking is not a necessary practice. Criticizing or slamming another musician's performing ability is petty and makes you appear small, narrow-minded, and insecure. However, you could view the competitive factor on a much broader scale, with the understanding that the very nature of the entertainment and music industry is itself competitive. It's smart to keep a watchful eye out for popular industry trends and try to make your act "competitive" in the sense of "equally marketable." You can show independence and confidence by exercising your own bold and assertive individuality, often recognized as appealing attributes that are far from abundant.

**Quick Onstage
Confidence Builders**

Remember these simple confidence builders the next time you're on stage.

- It takes a lot of nerve to be where you are right now, and you've got it.

- More than half of your audience would be scared lifeless to be standing where you are. How many of them could do what you're doing right now?

- You've practiced and you know your instrument.

- If someone doesn't like the way you play, so what—someone else will.

- A fellow musician who is openly critical of your performance ability may in fact be envious or intimidated by you.

- Who's got the gig, and who is sitting out in the audience?

- Close your eyes and imagine that you're in your own living room.

- Focus on outdoing your own last performance.

- Don't solicit opinions of your performance from the audience.

 *You must be confident enough to show respect for fellow musicians at all levels of proficiency.*

MAINTAIN YOUR OWN IDENTITY

It's important not to let your identity become buried within the structure of a band, because one day you may wish to reclaim it. Always remember, you were an individual with independent goals going into the band. You must try not to lose that idea if your band breaks up. Start writing down your own personal goals for each upcoming year. List things that you and only you would like to achieve and occasionally remind yourself as needed. You must never forget who you are before, during, and after your involvement with any band. Maintain your own personal bio and plan a course of action should your band come to a sudden demise.

In my own experience, the unexpected breakup of my band, the After Five Band, was a challenge to recover from. It left me feeling as if I'd been pushed off a moving train and was a terrific blow to my ego, my self-confidence, and my music career. With no course of action prepared, I was forced to become the most dynamic performer I could.

To survive in the music scene, you must nurture your own unique identity. Now when I perform, whether solo or as part of a band, my identity stays intact and the audience perceives me as an independent artist with my own personal appeal. Maintaining your identity allows you to be a more confident and compelling performer, which can in turn make your a greater asset to your band.

You may not realize it now but your personality could be even more valuable, with more money-making potential, on its own than as part of a band. By constraining your talents and personal identity exclusively within a band you could do yourself a great injustice and severely limit your own music-career possibilities.

Tips to Help You Maintain Your Own Identity

- Play other gigs as a sideman with other musicians.

- Develop your own solo routine until you have enough songs to do at least a three-hour set. You can develop this routine at your own pace without the pressure of soliciting gigs while still performing with your own band. Drummers can try a duo or small combo routine.

- If you are starting a new act, use your own name somewhere in the name of the band, like "the John Slate Band" or "Rumble, featuring John Slate."

- Write and maintain your personal bio, listing your own achievements.

- Network with important contacts you meet during your involvement with a band, and stay in touch with them. Make these people aware of your status if your band breaks up.

These suggestions are not intended to motivate selfish acts to benefit only yourself but to secure your identity as an individual and increase your options as an independent performing artist.

HOW STRESS CAN AFFECT YOUR WORK

I remember one summer when work was exceptionally slow. I was behind on bills and had no gigs on my calendar. Tension at home had become pretty high. I found myself snapping at my wife and children for little or no reason. Although I generally consider myself a levelheaded individual who works well under pressure, during this period things had become almost unbearable. I began to realize that my stress was spilling over into my relationships with potential clients, as well. When a prospect would call asking about my availability on a specific date, and their final decision was based on inquiring with other bands, my tolerance level was low. I found myself breaking the number-one rule of negotiating: "Don't appear too eager."

Once, I had a meeting with an interested prospect and delivered my contract, but it was not signed nor was a deposit secured, so our arrangements were left in a pending state. Because this was a corporate entity, and a senior executive had requested that I perform on the date in question, my contract and price proposal had to go through a chain of command and under the close scrutiny of elected community members. The senior executive, who was also an acquaintance, brought to my attention that the company's receptionist felt that I had been rude on the phone. After being made aware of this, I made a point to call the receptionist and apologize, realizing that the stress of my desperate situation had been reflected in my voice without my even knowing it. I was about to crack.

Some people have an inclination toward unnecessary stress: some are workaholics, overly committed to their work or an assortment of unrelated activities, while others are perfectionists obsessed with details. As if working as a musician isn't challenging enough, the anxiety over simply preparing for a gig can take its toll on many of us. Stress is a real concern and, if uncontrolled, can result in an unhappy life or severe health problems.

Everyone has a different level of tolerance for stress. When you find yourself under pressure, take a break and distance yourself from your work for a while. Consider having a spouse or significant other take phone calls for bookings and relay the information to you. You might even consider re-evaluating your entire situation and make the decision to either tough it out or find a day-gig (regular employment) to help ease financial stress.

Check It Out! ▶ *Making your living as a performing artist can be very difficult and stressful at times. How well can you handle stress and pressure? Do you buckle under the slightest tension, or can you endure under the toughest of situations?*

A Few Tips to Help Eliminate Unnecessary Stress on the Gig

- Arrive in plenty of time to set up and relax before your performance.

- Prepare costumes or other clothing the day before an engagement.

- Make sure your vehicle is fueled up and maintenance is done at least one day before your gig.

- Avoid coffee, tea, and other sources of caffeine just before a performance.

- Allow yourself a few moments of quite time to meditate and reflect several hours before an engagement.

- Avoid getting into arguments before leaving for a gig.

- Wear clothing that you are comfortable in.

- Never wear tight shoes; break in new shoes before wearing them to a gig.

- Don't look at your phone and electric bills just before leaving for a gig.

- If you must travel a great distance from home, leave early enough so you can drive at a relaxed speed.

- Make sure you bring directions to the gig, including a map if necessary. Also, have the phone number of the key person within reach.

- Prepare a set list so you don't have to wing it.

- The early years of your music career will be guided mostly by trial and error.

- Don't set unrealistic goals, and by all means, don't procrastinate.

- The more options you give yourself, the more likely you are to make your dreams become a reality.

- It's important not to let your identity become buried within the structure of a band.

- You should maintain your own personal bio and determine what course of action you will take in the event that your band comes to a demise.

- With the introduction of MIDI (musical instrument digital interface), there are many new possibilities for performers and recording artists who might never have been able to enter the music industry any other way.

- When booking gigs, you must be creative and persistent.

- A good musician will always appreciate the support of other musicians.

- Build emotional support factors by including your significant other in your endeavors.

- Learn to think like a professional.

CHAPTER 2

Laying the Foundation for a Successful Music Career

I t's true that your music career is, in essence, an entrepreneurial endeavor with various risks resting on your shoulders. Your role as a musician/entrepreneur will be met with envy by most working-class individuals who gripe about having to punch a time clock or how their hours were cut with no chance for overtime this week. The independent musician is afforded the opportunity to work at a seemingly leisurely pace. Evenings performing in clubs and restaurants are often perceived by the general public as relaxation and self-gratification. Consequently, through no fault of their own, nonmusicians may not appreciate the hidden infrastructure around which your music career is built. In this section we'll look at some of the underlying fundamentals and responsibilities of organizing the basic business structure of your music career.

ORGANIZING YOUR BUSINESS

Managing a music career haphazardly or with little foresight can become a costly and ultimately unproductive venture. But the self-reliant and aware musician can avert unnecessary and debilitating pitfalls. Without a doubt, a band is a business; strip away its outer shell, and the primary structure and working components are revealed.

After deciding on a name, your first consideration should be what category the band's business structure falls under. There are several to choose from: sole proprietor, partnership, corporation, limited liability partnership, limited liability corporation, etc. Speak with your tax advisor or a CPA to assist you in selecting the best method for structuring your business based on your individual circumstances and state requirements.

You can establish a bookkeeping system by opening a basic checking account, solely for the purpose of tracking earning and expenses. To reduce confusion, open a checking account under the band's working name and pay band members exclusively through this account. Your bank can help you decide on the best account options.

If you own a computer, obtain bookkeeping software, such as *Quicken*, or something that is specific to the task of tracking schedules, earnings, and expenses for working bands and musicians. (One such program is *Gig-O-Rama*, which I developed myself. You can download a free demo copy at www.giglogic.com, or get it by writing to Gig-O-Rama Software, P.O. Box 720913, Oklahoma City, OK 73172.)

In addition to word-of-mouth, the simplest means to or representing your new business image is with a business card. As a rule, your business card should give the public a general idea of what your business or service is without being cluttered or too wordy. Adding a logo or unique design element makes for an eye-catching and artistically appealing card. A logo is a graphic image that captures your persona. However, standard clip art, such as staves or musical notes, can confine your band's image to a less-than-inspiring state of mediocrity.

Avoid becoming overly concerned with card design to the point of deterring progress. Your name, address, phone number, and fax number, e-mail address, or Web-site URL are sufficient. You may be tempted to change your graphic image as your band settles into a more established position, but if possible, keep your business card, letterhead and envelopes consistent and uniform, with the same look and basic design theme.Conflicting or inconsistent information can create confusion for your clients and prospects.

Another item to consider is a postcard. The postcard adds a very professional touch to any business. Use it to inform fans where and when your band is playing or as a convenient way to correspond with a prospect or client to convey a simple idea. *Don't* use a postcard to send confidential business information. For less expensive postage rates, it's best to use standard sizes. Current postal regulations require your postcards to be no larger than 4¼ by 6 inches and no smaller than 3½ by 5 inches. If you need more information, ask your local postmaster for a detailed breakdown of postcard dimension and size requirements.

Recognize that you are a small business with all the growth potential of your large, corporate counterparts. Being a small, home-based business affords you room to grow at your own pace without the added pressure of maintaining expensive office space. Today, home-based businesses are widely accepted, and when set up correctly the designated area can be included as a yearly tax deduction. A secluded area of your home or apartment is suitable in the absence of a spare room. You may also consider a small corner of your bedroom as a modest work area. Here you have the benefit of privacy away from the interruptions of household activities while speaking with a prospect or client over the phone.

Without question, your phone line should be equipped with an answering machine that includes a brief outgoing message. Little compares to the frustration of listening to a 15-second musical interlude and a 20-second outgoing message before being able to leave your own message. If you begin to notice frequent hang-ups on your machine, your outgoing message might be too lengthy, awkward, or simply annoying.

A fax machine is another useful tool that will prove invaluable when someone needs a copy of your bio or other important document in a hurry. A personal computer should be at the top of your wish list. It is the single most important tool your home office will need, capable of a multiplicity of functions.

Remember, if you don't already own office equipment, it's not always necessary to buy these items new. Watch the classified ad section of your local newspaper; the Sunday edition usually has best selection. Each week you will find an assortment of reasonably priced office equipment and other items at a fraction of their original costs. Auctions are another source for obtaining office equipment. You can also find a thorough listing of weekly auctions in the Sunday classifieds.

Below is a list of basic essentials you will need to run an efficient home office.

- A computer and printer, bookkeeping software, and fax modem for Internet access

- A desk (the dining-room table will work for now)

- A small filing cabinet

- A telephone

- A fax machine

- An answering machine (preferably digital)

- Business cards, stationery, and letterhead.

- A full-size wall calendar (dry-erase is good)

  It may take you a while to accumulate all of these things. At this point, space should not be a primary concern—some of the world's most successful businesses started right at the kitchen table. Did you know that Apple Computer started in a garage?

  The following is a list of basic outside resources to help make your new home office a success.

- Good transportation

- A checking account

- A P.O. Box or other stable address (avoid using an apartment address for business if possible)

- A reliable, professional printing service

- A dependable tax adviser

- A pager (optional)

OPTIMIZE YOUR PERSONAL PRODUCTIVITY

It has been said that "idleness is the holiday for fools." Curiously, the author of that statement will forever remain anonymous. I discovered it in a fortune cookie while dining at a Chinese restaurant, and I was inspired by it's truth and wisdom.

Before conducting any activity each day, or before retiring for the evening the night before, take a few moments to compose a brief list of things to do that day, carefully listing them in order of importance. List only those tasks that can realistically be accomplished within the course of one day, and then follow through with each one before moving on to the next.

Set Deadlines

In essence, deadlines are nothing more than a series of short-term goals set with the intention of completing each task at hand by a particular date. When you set deadlines and meet them on time, your productivity will steadily increase along with your personal efficiency. You can apply the following steps to enhance your own personal productivity and meet established deadlines:

- Routinely write a list of all your current projects.

- Number the items in your list arranging them in order of importance and including deadlines for each. (Be sure to give yourself realistic time constraints).

- Decide which projects can be deleted and continued at a later date.

- Starting with the highest-priority item, complete each one before moving to the next.

The key to meeting deadlines is not to overwhelm yourself with too many projects at once. Organization will play a powerful role in your overall success. The unorganized musician is often plagued by procrastination, which can bring personal productivity to a virtual standstill. The overall effects can be devastating, denying any sense of accomplishment or direction.

Work on Communication

In addition to organizing projects, concentrate on your ability to organize your thoughts when communicating with others. As you develop your own business routine or general working structure don't overlook the importance of communicating intelligently and effectively—this is the very foundation of your success potential.

Eventually you will be required to draft a letter or brief memo. For a lot of musicians, writing a letter or sending a postcard is a rare practice. Being self-conscious about my own handwriting, the oddest things go through my mind when I'm faced with this task. Exactly how will the receiver analyze my handwriting? If I write too large I might come across as bold or overconfident, but writing too small might convey a passive, weak, or emotionally unstable personality. Just about everybody has some sort of hang-up regarding their own communications shortcomings, especially when it comes to asking somebody for something. It could be weak vocabulary skills or an inability to pronounce particular words correctly. We're all bound to human frailties; this is part of our world, and it's very acceptable. However, you must learn to communicate your thoughts on many levels with intelligence and articulation.

The Internet has swiftly become the next most common means of informal communication after the telephone. E-mail is an accepted and growing form of communication for business, and it doesn't require the formal structure of a business letter. Along with the casual persona e-mail offers, one can attach an assortment of files, including text, graphic, MIDI, and audio files, to be sent instantaneously to a party on the other side of the world.

There's Something to be Said about Networking

Has your band ever been hired for a gig because someone referred you to them? If so, that is a direct result of networking. You can start building your network by exchanging business cards, phone numbers, and other useful information every time you meet someone associated with the music business. Whenever you meet someone, ask yourself, "How can this person help me reach my goal?" Engage them in conversation, and ask questions so you can get an idea of what resources that person possesses that may someday benefit you.

Of course, networking doesn't just work one way—you must also be willing to be a resource for others. Routine interaction with other motivated people will greatly expand your opportunities and expedite your career objectives and goals.

Networking is the most important aspect of managing your own music career. It is a true form of independence and it should be among your highest priorities. Meet as many people as you can. Create a new database just for this purpose and maintain contact with those people.

If you don't have a manager or an agent and must represent yourself or your band, it is extremely important to project and maintain a professional and polished image at all times.

As with anything, representing yourself has its advantages and disadvantages. Dealing with a client or prospect on your own behalf can give you the image of being small-time; price negotiation will be a keen issue, as your fee will be more readily challenged. On the other hand, your personal involvement ensures that you know how a deal is handled. It allows you to make immediate decisions when negotiating fees and terms, instead of having an agent tell your prospect, "Let me get back to you on that."

Given time and experience, you will eventually gain a feel for self-management and enjoy the flexibility of negotiating prices without compromising earnings due to an agent's fee. Self-management does, however, place the entire burden of responsibility on you. Representing yourself will require confidence, creativity, and an overall general aptitude to handle the daily business tasks that are separate from your involvement as a musician. If you decide to manage yourself, exploit the decision fully. Decide on a name for your personal management entity. You could choose to use your own name, like "Maurice Johnson Management." Delegate management duties to band or family members. Be sure to have business cards, letterhead, and envelopes printed up with your personal management name. Include the name and a logo on fax cover sheets and all important documents.

Running your own business will attract a variety of enterprising people all too eager to propose an assortment of money-making schemes to you. This is a natural inclination and the mechanism through which a significant number of contacts are derived. But look cautiously at the individual who approaches you in a club setting, someone you don't know who wants to discuss a business venture. Take it upon yourself to investigate anyone who says they can promote you or make you money. If you're ever asked to make a personal financial investment, confer with an attorney or disregard the proposition. Unfortunately, there are no guaranteed get-rich-quick schemes in the music business. You have chosen one of the most competitive, stressful, and demanding trades. Your ultimate success depends solely on your personal hard work and perseverance. Always remember that no one will give you anything without a price. As you become more knowledgeable about business dealings, your ability to make good judgment calls will increase.

Avoid conducting business in a setting where there are many distractions. Sometimes you'll be approached by someone in a situation or environment where the last thing on your mind is discussing business. Being in the music business often places me in a club or restaurant where there is live entertainment. On many occasions during my personal leisure time I run into an attorney friend. Our mutual interest in assorted business ventures usually turns our conversation in that direction, even as we remind each other that we should not mix business with pleasure. But conflicting schedules may make it next to impossible to meet in normal business settings during normal business hours. Once, recognizing our dilemma, he suggested that the next time we see each other out we just go somewhere to have coffee and discuss our grandiose ideas, but we both know that the chances of that happening on a weekend night are zero. Now, as a private joke between us, every time we run into one another at a club, we stop and exclaim jokingly, "Let's have coffee!" and laugh our heads off, leaving everyone around us totally perplexed.

As a general rule, when it's time to discuss serious business ideas, avoid the distraction of a club or other environment that doesn't allow you to focus your full attention on important matters at hand.

INSURANCE FOR THE SELF-EMPLOYED MUSICIAN

Some insurance agencies do offer affordable medical coverage for the self-employed musician. In many cases, such policies require a higher deductible in order to keep a low monthly premium. For most musicians, a stay in the hospital could be financially devastating, with all the added expenses to cover a variety of services a hospital must provide during your stay. Look for a policy that covers hospitalization, intensive care, extended care, accidental injury, and inpatient and outpatient surgery. Ask several insurance agencies about policies that offer these benefits with a low monthly premium.

Musical equipment is usually covered by renters' or homeowners' insurance. These are common, inexpensive policies offered by most insurance agencies, and they can protect your hard-earned investments against theft, fire, or destruction. The first thing to do is to make an inventory list of every piece of musical equipment you own, along with other important household items of value. Your inventory list should include the make, model, and serial number of each thing on your list. It is very important that you keep good documentation on all items. Make a note of any outstanding characteristics of each, such as a keyboard with a chipped F key. Take photos of all items and make sure they are clear enough to show identifying details, because it is highly unlikely that many of the items you own are one of a kind. So don't photograph your equipment from too great a distance; get close enough to read the make and model numbers. After you have completed your inventory list and photographs, file them away in a safe place. If you have a safety deposit box, keep important files there as an extra precaution, in case of fire.

TAX CONCERNS FOR THE WORKING MUSICIAN

A working musician, band, or any other performing artist is subject to the same laws and regulations as any other taxpayer. All of the deductions available to other small businesses are available to musicians, as well.

Take into consideration the type of business entity you or your band has chosen for conducting business. There are several options, as mentioned above. Each of these selections has advantages and disadvantages, depending on your unique circumstances, and affects the way you report your taxes.

Typically, musicians are recognized as independent contractors, in which case you should report to the IRS using Form 1099, Miscellaneous Income. Make sure each band member who has been paid $600 or more during the year has one of these forms. When you work as an independent contractor, no tax withholdings are required on the part of your employers. In some cases, when long-term engagements apply, the party that hires you—a client, restaurant, club owner, etc.—may require or request withholding taxes. This alters your status from independent contractor to employee, in which case you are eligible for the full benefit package offered by the employer.

Other business entities mentioned above (excluding a sole proprietorship or subcontractor) would need to file taxes using Schedule K. Each entity would issue individual partners and shareholders this form to be filed along with their personal taxes. Talk to your tax adviser to find out which forms are appropriate for you.

Common Tax Deductions for Musicians and Performing Artists

- Depreciation on equipment and instruments

- Cost of clothing, dry cleaning, etc. (only if your act requires a uniform or costume)

- Automobile expenses—deducted either by the actual-expense method or by the mileage method

- Equipment and services for business operation and promotion: computers, photocopies, office supplies, advertising, printing, etc.

- Rent for (home-) office space and a percentage of utilities

These are general and common areas of concern that should not be overlooked. Above all, you must realize that you are running a business, so be careful to keep track of band expenses as you would with any other business. Find a good tax advisor who understands your business, and work very closely with that individual to meet all of the reporting requirements. Take advantage of all available tax deductions for yourself or your band.

Check It Out! *All business structures are only routine formalities upon which to build. Your band's overall success and growth potential ultimately depend on tenacity, continued ability to deliver a salable performance, and regularly applying newly acquired knowledge from many sources.*

- Your music a career is an entrepreneurial endeavor.

- Set realistic goals and deadlines.

- Organization will play a significant role in your overall personal success as an independent musician/entrepreneur.

- If you manage yourself or your band, it is extremely important to project and maintain a professional and polished image at all times.

- Avoid discussing business in non–business settings.

- Your musical equipment can usually be covered by a renters' or home-owners' insurance policy.

- Check with your tax consultant to find out how to report your income tax and what tax deductions you are eligible for.

CHAPTER 3

Building Your Band

W hile the term *band* implies more than one person, your band as a whole must function as a single entity. The way band members seem to lock in with each other during a stage performance with almost effortless, flawless unity is known as "chemistry." Some bands have it naturally, while others have to really work at it. Chemistry is an important attribute that many record labels, promoters and even your audience will look for. Your band should be an organization that routinely exercises discipline and sincere effort directed toward a common goal.

FINDING MUSICIANS

Depending on the area where you live, finding other musicians to start a band may not be a difficult process. Word of mouth is at the top of the list when dealing with musicians in your general area. Music-store bulletin boards run a close second among the popular sources. Most music stores maintain a bulletin board where musicians can post fliers, business cards, and notices for musicians looking for bands and bands looking for musicians. Take time to write your own brief notice that says that you are starting a band and seeking musicians who can perform.

Here's an example: "Starting a new alternative rock band. Looking for bass player, drummer, keyboardist, female and male vocalist. Must be professional and willing to rehearse. Must have own song list." Include your phone number printed clearly and large enough to be easily seen. State your message in as few words as possible. After you've seen the local music-store bulletin boards (especially those that are not cleared regularly) you may begin to notice a chaotic paper pileup. Eager musicians compete for visible space in order to ensure that their card or flier will be seen on top of the pile. This will be your biggest challenge when using bulletin boards. Despite this, bulletin boards remain a good method for locating musicians.

Most every city has at least one publication that promotes and highlights local clubs and restaurants offering entertainment. The classified sections of these publications usually have a musicians' market section. Some of them offer free listings for musicians looking for other musicians.

MUSICIAN TYPES

The following portraits reveal a glimpse of common musician personalities that you are likely to encounter at some point in your music career. We all harbor a little of each of these in our own characters. When we begin to favor one particular trait, complications can occur.

Intimidated

Often the band member who's intimidated or just plain afraid will use the excuse, "We're not ready yet," and have your band rehearsing the same songs for a year or more. Fear and insecurity like this can become a barrier for your band that will most likely create frustration and stifle the band's growth.

Egotistical

You can bet the egotistical musician has nothing to fear but you and every other musician who threatens to steal her glory. Her natural defense is to shield herself behind the veil of an overexaggerated display of confidence. As a fellow band member, you're best off trying to understand this nature and overlook it.

Self-Centered

A band member who is unwilling to participate in a team effort can be a detriment to the band as a whole. It's only fair for the entire band to benefit from any activities or business dealings conducted under the band's name. One or more band member should never conduct business in seclusion or secrecy, without the entire band's knowledge or participation.

Gung-Ho

Always ready to jump at any and every opportunity, the gung-ho musician is impulsive and bold and generally doesn't know or care to know about details or consequences. A gung-ho personality is probably not the best choice for a bandleader but makes an excellent candidate for a band member.

The Perfectionist

The perfectionist feels that everything has to be just right. The right equipment, the right songs, countless rehearsals....Usually such individuals are, in fact, either musical geniuses, with a very critical ear and high musical standards, or simply petrified at the mere thought of performing and making mistakes in front of a live audience—or perhaps both.

CHOOSING THE RIGHT LEADER FOR YOUR BAND

Although a band is a collective effort, it helps nonetheless to have a designated leader. The bandleader's primary functions are to help maintain a sense of organization in the group and act as the main contact with whom prospects and clients conduct business.

New bands might not have an established leader. Choosing one among you to be leader can be done by a vote, or maybe one of you possesses natural leadership qualities. Generally the most outgoing individual will make a good choice as a leader. Sometimes your audience will make the choice for you. The singer is the one person whose voice is most heard and often appears to lead the band when selecting songs. If your band hasn't selected a primary representative, then you yourself may want to consider the position; that you're reading this book is a good indication that you have some sense of responsibility and ambition.

Every member of your band should take some responsibility for the betterment of the group. I remember my early days as a bandleader and the difficulty our group had with singers. To be quite honest, the problem was really a matter of resentment among the other members. Naturally, everyone was responsible for their own equipment, and rightfully so. As for our vocalist, his equipment was nothing but a microphone. Much to our dismay, his duties entailed merely rolling up a mic cord and carefully placing it into his gig bag, and in a flash he would disappear. All right, we thought he was lazy and tacky—but then again, he *was* a pretty good singer.

It takes the full cooperation of every band member for a band to run smoothly. Often there's one member who's good at public relations, another who is artistic, and so on. There are many factors outside of stage performance that make up a successful working band. Every member should share the extra responsibilities. At your next band meeting, suggest that each member, including yourself, be appointed a duty that best fits his skills.

Check It Out! *As a bandleader, any one of these personalities can be frustrating to work with. Whether your new band is composed of three musicians or ten, be honest with yourselves and select the most level-headed one among you, who has a good sense of business, to take the helm. Then try not to let egos cloud important decisions that can ultimately affect the success and progress of your band.*

MAKE THE MOST OF REHEARSAL TIME

Rehearsal time should be considered just as important as an actual gig. Whether you rehearse one or two days a week, be sure to choose a time that will not conflict with work schedules, school, or other activities that would prohibit any band member from attending a rehearsal. Establish a specific day of the week and a start and finish time for rehearsals, and stick with your schedule. Rehearsal is not a time for social gatherings. It should be treated seriously, with specific objectives in mind each time your band meets. Never bring friends or guests to a rehearsal. If your rehearsal takes place at a member's home, notify family members not to disturb you during that time. Your rehearsals should be goal oriented; whoever is in charge of selecting new songs should come to each rehearsal prepared with a list of specific songs to work on.

THE VARIETY BAND

A "variety band" is exactly what the name implies: a band that performs many kinds of music without leaning toward any particular style. Variety bands do keep busy and are often called upon, but the music industry places a low commercial value, if any at all, on this type of act. Depending on how far you'd like to take your band, and whether you're satisfied with playing country clubs, night clubs, private parties, etc., you may find that the variety band is a good choice. On the other hand, if you foresee entering the music scene on a larger scale—even to the point of seeking a record deal—a variety band might not be the way to go.

Whenever more than one person is involved in anything, there will be differences of opinion from time to time. The band that works closely together without an occasional quarrel is rare or even, I would venture to say, nonexistent. Sometimes you may have a band member who is never satisfied, is argumentative, and has a propensity for stirring things up. Although it may be difficult to pinpoint the nature of that person's problems, many of these differences of opinion can be settled by a simple vote.

 Many personality conflicts and misunderstandings can be kept at bay by signing a "partnership agreement" between band members. This agreement should spell out stipulations regarding the general operating structure of your band.

NOW THAT YOU'RE IN THE PUBLIC EYE

The trick to getting established locally is to make yourself as visible as possible. Whether you play solo or with a band, this is not as difficult as it sounds. You must first put some time and effort into creating a vehicle that will keep you in the public eye. With some thought and creativity, this can be done very effectively. You can start by posting fliers around town and calling friends and relatives to invite them out when you're playing.

As with anything new, there is a certain amount of awkwardness during a band's early development stages. It's kind of like wearing that new shirt your mom bought you for your birthday: it wasn't really your style, but after a while you got used to it. Don't expect everything to fall into place right from the start, even though it is possible. Have confidence in yourself, be persistent, and don't turn and run when someone says they're not interested.

It's funny how different people are. Have you ever noticed how certain people seem to have the ability to jump into a conversation with just about anyone? Those individuals have a strong, sometimes charismatic power of persuasion over others. Everybody sends out unique signals that others can sense. For example, most of us know when a person does or doesn't want to be approached. Being in the entertainment business naturally puts you in a position where people approach you often. With some practice and a little effort you can empower yourself with effective persuasion techniques that draw people to you. Start by learning to take advantage of those attributes you already possess. Make a conscious effort to show others that you can be approached; try giving them direct eye contact and a sincere smile, or make the first advance by greeting them. There's no big secret to being approachable—its called *personality.*

Check Ⅱ Out! ▶ *As you settle into a working routine, learn to anticipate the months to follow. It feels nice to have at least a couple of gigs each week, but what does next month's calendar look like? Try to stay at least two or three months ahead.*

A WORD ABOUT LEGAL REPRESENTATION

The need for legal representation depends on the scope of your band's endeavors. Bands that are engaged in recording and are looking for a record deal are good candidates for legal services.

New, up-and-coming bands that have caught the attention of a record label may have a hard time resisting the temptation to sign the first piece of paper set in front of them. Signing a record contract is no guarantee of success; it merely affords a band the opportunity to get their music distributed on a larger scale.

If you or your band is presented with a record contract, seek the aid of a competent entertainment lawyer. You can be sure that the record label that sent the contract has done the same, and their lawyer's job is to make sure that the contract leans heavily in their own favor. It only makes sense for you to have a lawyer look over your contract to decipher all the hidden clauses and provide you with some protection against signing away your rights. Never take a record label's contract at face value. Specific terms can be negotiated in order for the contract to work in your favor, as well as the record label's. Speak with musician friends who can refer you to an attorney, or contact the American Bar Association—whatever you do, find one.

You'll find more on this subject in Chapter 8, "Bits and Pieces." New York entertainment lawyer Wallace Collins supplies a healthy dose of inside information on the subjects of copyright, "works made for hire," and what to look for when shopping for an entertainment lawyer.

YOUR BASIC PRESS KIT

Be creative with your press kit, but keep it simple and uncluttered. It should include a bio, an 8 x 10–inch black-and-white glossy photo, a list of your fees, and a demo tape of four or five brief songs. Also be sure to include any newspaper or magazine write-ups about you or your band. A price list for your tapes, CDs, or other merchandise is optional; if you choose to include one, print it on a separate sheet in your press kit.

WRITING YOUR BIO

Composing a bio can be quite a challenge, especially if you're not used to writing and can't get someone else to write one for you. First, make a note of important points that you want to emphasize, and then take each point and add a little more detail. Be sure to include major accomplishments, endorsements, studio projects, and future goals. Write in the third person as if you are talking about someone else, avoiding the use of "I" and "me."

When you start, don't worry whether each point makes sense or relates to the others; this will all come together later. Your main concern now is recording your information on paper. Keep in mind that your bio is like a resume and will constantly change as your experience as a working musician grows.

The next step is to organize what you have written in chronological order, listing dates of more significant events. Think of it as taking the reader through a mini tour of your life as a musician, from start to present, occasionally inserting a date to give perspective.

MAKING YOUR PROMOTIONAL MATERIAL LOOK GOOD

Your unique attributes and charismatic personality set you apart from everyone else. These aspects, combined with a certain mystique from your public not knowing the full scope of your potential or social contributions, help to heighten and enhance your public image. The way you present your persona can help raise the stakes when people are considering employing your services.

The general public will view you from many angles outside of your stage performance. The way you dress says a lot about you. Your vocabulary, the type of car you drive, your smile, your business card—many things affect how you're perceived by the public.

Your persona on paper is equally as important as personal interaction. A poor graphic representation can result in a misconception of you by potential fans. Think about how much time and effort you spend grooming before a gig: you comb your hair, straighten your jacket, and polish your shoes; you don't just step right out of bed and onto the stage. You should give just as much time, care, and attention to producing graphics and other promotional materials.

Something as simple as a flier deserves close attention to balance, good taste, and creativity. The design and printing process of your business cards, fliers, and posters should all be well thought out. Over the years I have watched people with good intentions waste money printing items that could have used more work in the design stage. I can't teach you how to become an outstanding graphic artist, but I can tell you how to use good sense and judgment in basic design and layout to help save you money and also make a good first impression.

Tips for Producing Effective Graphics

- Don't clutter the page. Too many visuals can cause the reader's eyes to wander and not focus on anything.

- Use no more than three fonts on a page.

- Avoid excessive use of upper-case text.

- Don't use script or other overly ornate, hard-to-read type styles.

- Place objects so they draw attention toward the middle of the page instead of outward. For example, if you use a picture of a person's face, position it so that they're looking toward the center.

- Stick with common paper sizes (8½" x 11", 11" x 17", etc.)

- Work with a printer whom you know and trust or ask other musicians to refer you to one.

- Leave certain things, such as color separation and digital photo editing, to a professional.

- Try to share some of the work load.

- If you can't afford to do it right, don't do it.

Check Ⅱ Out! ▶ *Your appearance is judged not only by the clothes you wear but just as importantly by your graphic representation. Throughout your career as a musician/performing artist, you will need to depict your image graphically in one form or another. Do it with style, good taste, and creativity.*

TAKE ADVANTAGE OF YOUR LOCAL PRESS

Whatever you do, stay in good standing with your local press. Make a monthly schedule of performance dates and either mail, fax, or personally deliver it to the entertainment editor of your local newspaper and every entertainment publication in your area. If you take full advantage of them, these publications can become the pulse of your advertising efforts, often requiring little or no money. You would do yourself a great disservice not to take advantage of this low-cost option. Be sure each publication has your photo (preferably black and white) on file. Send each one an updated photo as they become available. Routinely share newsworthy events that you, your band, or another band member have participated in. Invite the press to attend special functions or occasionally send out a promotional postcard.

GENERATE HYPE

Here's where you get to show off all that creative flair you've been holding back. Have you ever noticed how excited you feel when you hear that your favorite band is coming to your city? That excitement is generated by media hype. Fast-talking radio announcers, television ads, newspaper ads, word of mouth—all of this is meant to send you and all your friends running to the ticket booths. And it works!

Your band can create hype too, even if on a slightly smaller scale. Let's say most of your friends and local music fans have already seen you play. Your creative instinct tells you that you need to cook up something that will make the public want to come and hear your band again. *Now* would be a good time to announce a party to raise money for your band's new CD project, or maybe host a charitable fund-raiser for a worthy cause. These are just two examples; there are endless possibilities. The idea is to make a little sound like a lot, or better yet, make a lot sound like even more. If you put your mind to it, you can dream up many fresh ideas to draw attention.

Sometimes a laid-back approach works best. This means that you create hype only when you need it. Keeping your band's image hyped up all the time doesn't allow room for dynamics. A good band that keeps a low profile most of the time can keep fans eagerly anticipating their next big move.

GOING INTO THE STUDIO

After your band has played for a while and cultivated a unique sound and growing audience, it's time to record and explore new marketing possibilities. Your time in the studio should be well thought out. Make sure your band realizes and agrees on the purpose for going into the studio. Some bands just want to hear what they sound like on tape or choose to produce a demo solely for the purpose of booking gigs more easily. You may consider producing a professional recording and shopping it around to record labels. Whatever your reason, make sure you go into the studio with a purpose.

Many bands invest much time, hard-earned money, and sweat on a recording project that lasts six months, only to send a mere handful of tapes to a few record labels. The scenario usually goes like this. Either your band has saved money from gigs or someone loans it to them, and six months to a year later you finish a recording. You have 500 to 1,000 tapes and CDs made. The excitement of having your first recording dies down as your band becomes the local heroes to a few diehard followers. You might sell about 100 tapes to friends, family and fans. Ten of them, at the most, went to record labels with no positive response or none at all. By then you've lost interest in the project and feel that the music is old because you've heard each song at least a thousand times and could choke the next person who tells you they listen to it over and over in the car, at work, and at home. You then have about 700 tapes and CDs left over, and you're wondering how you're ever going to sell them all to recoup your investment. Before long, you're eager to start on the next project and do it all over again.

Any time you choose to invest in a professionally produced CD that you ultimately want to send out to record labels, it's best to order a small number of units. By pressing small quantities at a time, you can focus on sending your demo out to record labels as needed without incurring the expense of hundreds of CDs that might not sell fast enough to make the effort worthwhile. Rather than having a large pressing plant manufacture your CDs, try to find an individual or small facility that will burn about a dozen for you to send out to record labels.

Having a tape or CD that was not picked up by a record label is not the end of the world. A recording in any form, whether cassette or CD, is a plus for any band. A professional recording can be used to generate extra money for the band or as an advertising promotional spot for club appearances.

PLAN A COST-EFFECTIVE LIVE RECORDING PROJECT

Cost is a primary concern for a band that has little or no working capital. Rather than undertaking a big studio recording project, consider having someone with some basic recording equipment come out to one of your gigs and record an evening of your band's performance. A live recording can be a big seller right from the stage during your gigs. The money that you generate through tape sales can then be used to fund a studio project.

One of the easiest methods for recording live is with a simple two-mic setup. However, this technique works best with a solo act or small combo in a small, intimate setting. Recording in larger clubs may require more professional equipment and personnel, especially if you're recording a large band. Louder acts, such as rock or R&B, may require taking a direct line signal through a mixing board.

Once you've made your recording, you can then take your tape to a studio and have it edited. The editing process should consist of simply fading songs in and out, rearranging the order and length of songs, and making sure the overall volume is consistent throughout your tape. You can even add sampled applause with a keyboard or sound module.

Besides selling an inexpensively made live recording or other merchandise, look into the following options for raising money to pay for studio time.

Family and Friends

Your most immediate source for financing a recording project may be right under your nose. First look to family and friends. Uncle Joe, who always brags to friends and strangers about his favorite niece or nephew's musical talents, might be a great starting point. Friends who feel that your musical talents show promise may come through and spring for a few hours of recording time.

A word of caution, though: borrowing money from friends and family can sometimes create tension in a relationship, as the lender may wonder when you are going to pay them back. Whatever type of deal you make with a family member or friend, draw up some type of outline or agreement that spells out how and when you intend to repay them and how much of a return they can expect on their investment. A 20% return is a good figure to offer, which means Uncle Joe will receive $600 for his $500 investment, earning a $100 profit.

Advance Tape Sales

This approach calls for some creative thinking. I wouldn't advise this for a new band or performer who doesn't have an established following. A following doesn't necessarily mean several hundred people; it can be as few as 5 to 25 individuals who are willing to contribute a small investment toward your cause. After you have made solid arrangements with a studio and duplication facility, you may consider advance tape sales. Advance sales are among the least stressful options when it comes to financing your recording project.

During your performances, announce to your audience that your band is preparing to record a tape or CD. Offer them the opportunity to place an advance order, and have them fill out a mailing list and write in the number of units they would like to purchase. Although some fans will want to wait to pay you when the recordings are ready, others may be willing to pay for their orders up front. It may surprise you to find a few faithful fans who will purchase several copies.

Club Sponsors

This is a clever method that can generate good results for both you and a club owner. Present the idea that you would like to stage a live recording session in a club. If the owner seems agreeable, continue by explaining how the establishment could gain publicity if it promoted the event as a special evening. Then pitch your real proposition: that in exchange for the club covering the cost of your recording session or the duplication service (whichever is greater) you will name the finished recording after the club, for example, *Maurice Johnson Live! at the Hot Spot*. Offer to write a brief description of the club within the package, or you could even have the club owner write the liner notes for your finished product. A club can benefit greatly from having an album named after it, especially if the recording becomes popular. As the CD or tape travels through the hands of new listeners throughout the country, the club's name will become a central focus for visitors from out of town, who will seek out this exciting hot spot for entertainment.

WHAT DID WE LEARN?

- Your band or group has to function as a single entity.

- Your band should be an organization that routinely exercises discipline and sincere effort directed toward a common goal.

- You can use word of mouth and music store bulletin boards to find other musicians who may also want start a band.

- Every member in your band should share duties and responsibilities for bettering of the band.

- Rehearsal time should be considered just as important as an actual gig.

- Variety bands do keep busy and are often called upon, but a major draw back is the music industry places a low commercial value on this type of act if any at all.

- Your bio is like a resume and, over time, will go through many changes as your experience as a working musician grows.

- Your press kit should include a bio, an 8 by 10–inch, black and white glossy photo, and a demo tape.

- When writing your bio, avoid the use of "I or me" and organize facts in chronological order.

- It's important to have well-designed promotional material.

- Whatever you do, stay in good standing with your local press, and generate hype to keep yourself visible.

- Recording live can be a cost-effective way to produce a tape or CD.

Pricing Your Performances

Pricing is more a state of mind than a matter of numbers. This is clearly demonstrated with so-called "collectible" or "exclusive" items. Collectibles are usually attainable only in limited quantities and have prospective buyers willing to pay almost any price for them. I once learned of a wealthy New Jersey guitar collector who purchased a one-of-a-kind 1958 D'Angelico arch-top guitar, which originally sold for a mere $400, for $150,000. One week later, another collector offered him $300,000 for the same guitar, but he turned the offer down.

An exclusive item or service is available only through a single or limited source. For the working musician, exclusivity is an asset when it comes to setting and negotiating a comfortable price. In this section you'll learn that it takes more than a calculator to formulate pricing strategies that both you and your client can live with.

SIX CATEGORIES OF PRICING

Pricing can range from simple to complex. Determining a price for your band or an individual performance should be more than a fleeting formality just to be hurriedly brushed aside. When quoting your fee to a prospect, your method of arriving at an agreeable price will fall into one or more of the following six categories:

Comparison

Comparing to the amount other bands charge for similar gigs, based on an informal survey.

Calculation

Determining by a mathematical equation, often based on hourly rates.

Negotiation

Arriving at a compromise; this is generally the best approach for all parties concerned, giving both you and your prospect some control over the outcome.

Assessment of Self-Worth

Influenced by emotion, basing your decision on what you think you're worth; everyone's concept of self-worth is different.

Passive Acceptance

Accepting a prospect's offer without contest; you have no say under these conditions.

Obituary

Determining a figure without any preconceived foundation or logical formula.

THE "STANDARD PAY SCALE" ILLUSION

Some musicians believe it takes a lot of nerve to ask for more than a club, organization, or individual will likely offer to pay, when in fact it only takes confidence in knowing what you're worth and sticking to it. It's no big sin to challenge someone's entertainment budget. Occasionally holding your ground may mean you won't get booked for a particular gig, but step back and look at it—do you want to play that type of gig anyway? I have turned down some gigs because of principle, not pride. At times, I have contended with responses like, "So-and-so plays here all the time, and we only pay him such-and-such." I refuse to let other musicians' pay standards become *my* pay standards. It's a matter of principle. I have always fostered a "pay me what I'm worth" attitude.

If you feel that you're worth more than the "standard" pay scale (whatever that may be) that many establishments are willing to offer, remember that you have to prove it with *every* performance. Always exhibit your professionalism. Be confident and aggressive. Above all, don't be afraid to challenge the system by breaking the routine and asking for what you want, not what others have settled for.

Your minimum fee should represent the lowest price you are willing to accept. Once you have determined this, it is important not to make a habit of challenging it just to get a gig. By giving in to people who are unwilling to pay what you ask, your minimum fee becomes nothing more than a gate without a lock. Picture your minimum fee as the foundation upon which your house is built. You wouldn't go chipping away at its edges, would you?

To get a feel for what you should charge, look at what your competition charges by surveying at least three other local acts. This should be as simple as saying, "I'm starting a band and would like to know what your band charges." Be careful to avoid a competitive approach, as that is likely to send up a red flag and gain you false information, or none at all. Nonetheless, you will be surprised at the degree of price variation you'll hear. Now place yourself somewhere within the price brackets you've collected, or calculate the average by totaling up all the different prices and dividing by the number of bands in your survey, to get a general idea of what you intend to charge as a standard rate. Then decide on the lowest fee you are willing to accept. Here again, you can randomly pull out a figure within a realistic range or calculate a percentage of your normal price. This is your *minimum fee;* now stick with it.

When a prospect asks what your fee is, the way you respond is important. State your price with confidence. Realize that people read your body language: avoid holding your head down or looking away, which would indicate that you lack confidence or are untrustworthy. If you display a lack of confidence when stating your fee, the prospect is likely to challenge it with a lower figure.

Be sure to let your prospect know where your price breaks are. For instance, if your prices are based on a three-hour evening and your band is required to play for four hours, make the necessary price adjustment. You may want to charge a higher hourly fee for extra hours beyond your normal time frame.

WHEN TO AVOID ON-THE-SPOT PRICE QUOTES

You will notice that pricing for many of your engagements, such as at local clubs or basic wedding receptions, will require little or no calculation since you have already established standard and minimum prices for these. But be careful when quoting prices for less common bookings, such as corporate parties, nonlocal shows, and so on. For these engagements you should, at all cost, avoid making on-the-spot price quotes. Your prospect will have no trouble remembering the first price you quoted, especially if it was surprisingly lower than expected. Remember this simple rule of thumb: it's easier to lower your price than to increase it after you have already made a quote.

Every engagement has unique factors that affect pricing, and you should take the time to carefully calculate a fair price based on these things. Don't let a prospect pressure you into quoting a price immediately. Take their name and number and assure them that you will get back to them within a few days.

WRITTEN PRICE QUOTES

On occasion it will be necessary for you to submit a written price quote, sometimes referred to as a "price bid." One of the greatest benefits of a written quote is that it forces you to think about your price and eliminates any misunderstanding regarding your fee. Be sure to list performance times and total hours in your written price quote.

The formality of a written price quote submitted on your own personal letterhead, using one of your uniquely designed envelopes, will often impress a potential client. The fact that you are a musician is all the more reason to make every effort to project a professional image. Frankly, most people don't expect musicians to display a high level of professionalism or business smarts. Give yourself the upper hand by projecting a polished and professional image. Your prospect is likely to remember and respect your sharp sense of business, often with positive results.

Official organizations, such as schools and corporations, often require a contract before a check can be cut.

LOCAL PRICE SENSITIVITY

A good number of your former clients and current prospects may actually be acquainted with each other. This may become more evident as your band is referred to someone else by a previous client, indicating that there are personal links within your network of clients and prospects. When previous clients refer your band to someone else, it is likely that they will reveal the price you quoted to them. Uneven pricing can create friction and mistrust toward your band, which can greatly affect future engagements with previous clients. After you have been around for a while, having played parties and most of the local clubs, you will have been faced with many pricing options or alterations. Be aware of this and justify significant price variations when necessary. For example, a prospect might request that you include an additional band member for their function or perform longer than normal. Make it clear that these types of changes will affect pricing. When these conditions are made clear, extra charges should be acceptable.

BARGAIN PRICING

Sooner or later you will be approached by an acquaintance or a nonprofit organization, school, or institution that will ask for a price cut that is below your minimum fee. A request like this is usually accompanied by some explanation, like that there's a committee that only allows a budget of *x* dollars for entertainment and special functions.

I have, in most cases, stood my ground and stuck to my minimum fee. But when met with an unyielding and persistent prospect I have occasionally given in to a lesser fee—however, in these cases I was sure to impose a few of my own stipulations, such as doing a shorter performance or including some kind of barter trade. (I'll discuss barter more in a moment.)

 *Accept below-minimum prices only rarely, and ask your client to keep your fee arrangements confidential. Let your prospect know that you're doing her a favor, not the other way around.*

DEALING WITH NONLOCAL CLIENTS

Time and distance can dilute any details that you have arranged with your client, even to the point of enforcing critical terms like payment. When working with an out-of-state client, it's important to take detailed notes regarding all arrangements. Aside from filling out a contract, it may be necessary to attach an additional profile sheet to cover primary and secondary key persons, directions, and other specifics related to the engagement, such as load-in time and meal allowances.

Playing out of town or out of state usually means increased responsibility on your part, along with higher risks. Your price should reflect this. You may need to rent additional equipment or a van to haul both your gear and your band, incurring a higher cost that you should pass on to your client. You could calculate a travel fee based on mileage, or you could double or even triple your price. Ultimately, these arrangements are up to you. The bottom line is to make it worth your while.

In essence, greater distances mean greater risks. It's not considered tacky to ask for a 50% deposit for an out-of-state engagement. Your prospect will usually understand and might even want to prove his sincerity by offering a deposit without being asked.

 Be very sure to collect a nonrefundable deposit for any out-of-state engagement to offset your travel costs or serve as compensation should the client cancel.

PRYING A HIGHER PRICE FROM YOUR PROSPECT

A poker player never wants to show his hand for fear of losing to an opponent. Likewise, a money-conscious prospect's motive is to get you to quote a price before he makes an offer, in hopes that you'll quote a lesser figure. To turn the odds in your favor you can employ a similar tactic. There's no trick or psychological marvel to this, it only requires that you ask one question to set things in motion.

The initial idea is to make your prospect think within a higher price bracket. The technique is similar to that of selling a car. Knowing that a potential buyer will likely offer a lower figure, the seller deliberately sets an asking price much higher than the predetermined—but undisclosed—amount she actually wants to get for the car. As long as the buyer makes an offer at or above the seller's target price, everybody's happy; if the buyer agrees to the full asking price, then all the more profit for the seller. This technique, when applied to a prospect for a gig, may require a little daring and intuition on your part, because like the buyer of the car, a prospect will usually have a maximum figure already in mind.

Pay close attention to your prospect; observe what's different about that individual. In essence, all you're actually doing is sizing him up while speculating whether that person or his organization can afford an upscale price for your services. Listen closely to all the information your prospect gives you. Is it a private engagement for an individual or a large corporate entity? Or is it a fund-raiser for a charitable cause? These are important factors to consider as you begin to mentally calculate your asking fee.

Only after you've gathered all the necessary information, state your fee—but this time quote a price that is up to double your minimum fee. Listen carefully to how your prospect responds. Remember earlier when I said this technique requires that you ask one question? Well here it comes. If your prospect responds with something like, "I can't afford that," simply ask the question, *"What is your budget for this engagement?"* If their budget falls below your actual minimum fee (which you did not disclose), either offer to perform for a shorter period of time at that price or don't accept the engagement. On the other hand, if their budget falls slightly above your minimum fee you have two choices: you can accept the engagement, meaning the technique worked and you *did* get a higher fee than your minimum, or you can take a bold step and say, "We can do the engagement for *x*," with *x* being a sum slightly higher than their budget. Your prospect will pause and try to decide whether your services are worth a few extra dollars. At this point your negotiations are running strictly on intuition, so listen closely through the silence. (Of course, I must add that it helps to be preceded by a good reputation when you use this technique.)

Some people may view this as a strong-arm tactic, so don't expect a prospect to accept your initial price quote. But if they do accept it right off the bat, congratulations! All the more profit for you.

Check It Out! ▶ *If you find that many clients accept your higher price quote, it might be a good idea to increase your minimum fee and reevaluate your current standard prices.*

THE BARTER SYSTEM

You can use the barter system as an occasional option. Let's say your prospect wants to use your services but doesn't have the finances to hire you. Let's also say your prospect owns something of value that interests you and is willing to offer it in exchange for your services. That's barter—it's that simple, and people do it every day, in all levels of business. You may occasionally want to try barter during those rare times when money isn't a great concern. If a barter arrangement involves your band, make sure all the members agree to it and the entire band will benefit from it.

Remember that barter credits hold the same value as cash. If your cash fee is $200, you can barter for something of the same value. Since both parties agree on a fair trade value without exchanging money, the possibilities are limitless.

In my experience, I've had more barter opportunities working as a solo jazz guitarist than when working with a band. Think of barter in the same way as you think of playing merely for exposure: know where to draw the line. Most prospects would love to hire you under a barter agreement, but you could barter yourself into a cash-flow problem. I don't think your local grocer or utility company would accept a weekly serenade in exchange for their products or services!

- Studio recording time

- Printing and silk-screening

- Photography

- Equipment

- Legal services

- Advertising

- Club memberships

- Exclusive dining privileges

- Travel and flight arrangements

- Musical instruments

- Computers

- Cars

- Furniture

- Appliances

Did you know there are nationally recognized barter clubs? To find a barter-exchange club in any city, contact the local Chamber of Commerce. Barter is a unique and cost-effective form of trade recognized by prominent businesses and individuals.

#1

Would you believe that the very computer I used to write this book was obtained though the barter system? Here's how: A while back I had played some evening engagements for a new restaurant. One evening the owner made a point to tell me that he was in the computer business and currently built computers in his shop just below the restaurant. Knowing that his restaurant business wasn't doing so well, I offered to play jazz guitar during lunch hours for a few weeks in exchange for a new computer. After fulfilling both of our obligations, his restaurant gained a new image and I received a new, custom-built computer.

#2

Once, when I was performing in a family restaurant in Oklahoma City, a group of women got my attention and asked if I would consider playing in exchange for airline tickets. I later found out that one of them worked for a popular airline. Several months later, she called the restaurant where I had been performing in order to contact me. After reminding me about her offer of several months back, she explained her idea for a surprise birthday party for a friend that had previously stated that she would like me to perform for her birthday. It just so happened that I was planning a trip to California to attend a trade show a few weeks after her friend's birthday, so I agreed to perform for the party in exchange for round-trip tickets.

#3

Barter opportunities can present themselves at the most peculiar times. This one, unrelated to performing, was a complete surprise.

In another of my numerous entrepreneurial endeavors, my business partner and I needed to secure a trademark along with other expensive legal services. Through an acquaintance, I was introduced to a trademark and copyright attorney of a very prestigious firm. I attended a consultation with the attorney, assuming that I would get a list of outrageous fees for all the legal services our company was very much in need of but could never afford. I was correct in my assumption. Just before I left his office, the attorney looked at me and said, "For what it's worth, I would be pleased to represent your company in exchange for one of your exclusive products." Needless to say I was floored by his unexpected offer, and the rest is history.

#4

Here's one more unique barter story, which resulted from an unfortunate mishap. During the mid-1980s I had a pretty popular local band. After a two-year stint as the house band for a restaurant/club, we began booking private parties during the warm summer months. This particular engagement was a poolside celebration at an exclusive country club. As it was an outdoor party, our instruments and equipment were exposed to the elements of nature, such as the wind and rain. During this time I was playing a foreign-made copy of an expensive jazz guitar, and for the longest time I had wished that I could afford the expensive American version.

Everything had gone well so far, with no threat of rain. When it was time for the band to take a break, we all decided to go inside to cool off and get something cold to drink. I didn't think much about the mild breeze as I placed my guitar on the stand. When I returned, I noticed my guitar laying face down on the concrete, only to discover that the neck was busted, leaving me suddenly without an instrument to finish the gig, or play at all, for that matter. An audience member and acquaintance of the band saw my dilemma and responded with an assuring, "I'll be back in 20 minutes." He returned carrying a nice-looking guitar case that made me think there had to be something nice inside. This guitar turned out to be the expensive, American-made version of my now busted guitar. I was amazed when the man said, "It's yours, keep it—we'll work something out. By the way, my sister is getting married in July. Can we work a trade deal?" That wedding reception took place without a hitch. To top it off, this particular barter deal provided me with an expensive instrument less than an hour after my foreign copy was destroyed, while the other band members still got paid in cash.

WHAT DID WE LEARN?

- Make it a point to take some time to establish your standard and minimum fees.

- Your minimum fee represents the lowest price you will accept.

- Avoid making on-the-spot price quotes for less common bookings, such as annual corporate parties or nonlocal engagements.

- On occasion it will be necessary for you to submit a written price quote.

- A good number of your former clients and current prospects may be personally acquainted with each other and share your pricing information.

- Sooner or later you will be approached by either a general acquaintance, a non profit organization, school, or institution that will ask for a price below you minimum fee.

- If a barter arrangement involves your band make sure all members agree to it and the entire band will benefit from it.

- Use your intuition to get a higher price form a prospect.

CHAPTER 5

Working with Prospects and Clients

I n the everyday big-business world, proposals, business plans, contracts, demographic studies, cost analyses and the like are normal practice between corporate giants and their prospects and clients. When you shrink it down to a musician's perspective, your proposal is usually verbal, your business plan is your contract, and your demographic study is finding out who will hire you for how much money. A cost analysis can be as simple as figuring out how much you'll pay for equipment rental and a sound person compared to how much you'll earn for the evening. Any way you look at it, you're responsible for the sensitive balance between yourself and your prospects or clients. Take this role seriously and treat it with the same intensity and drive as your corporate-giant counterparts do.

Check It Out! ▶ *Business dealings, regardless of their nature, consist of many nuances and psychological factors. These factors can and will affect the outcome of a negotiation or any situation in which either party is expected to compromise. A sense of humor and lighthearted nature, although not appropriate in every business setting, can sometimes cut through stale and laborious formalities. Learn to employ this attitude whenever you can.*

ESTABLISH A PROFESSIONAL RELATIONSHIP

Your prospect or client will most likely also be your key person. The relationship you establish must be mutually pleasant and professional throughout the duration of your contract. Your initial impression will usually set the tone of your relationship with prospects and clients. When meeting with them, be aware of your demeanor and poise and be willing to make adjustments as necessary to allow them to feel comfortable. Always exercise appropriate, professional behavior. Flirtatious or condescending advances send messages that are confusing at best and ultimately damage a professional relationship.

Just because someone says they'd like your band to perform on a certain date for a specific price, "Mark this on your calendar" doesn't guarantee that the job is yours. As a rule of thumb, your prospect must commit to you by signing a contract and submitting a deposit.

Take extra precaution to get signed contracts from new clients. This includes gigs at wedding receptions, baby showers, birthday parties, and so on. A contract gives both parties a mutual sense of obligation and a means for possible recourse in the event of a legal dispute. A simple handshake may occasionally substitute for a contract with a known club or restaurant owner whose reputation and business ethics you know to be admirable and trustworthy. Nevertheless, a written contract is best for long-term engagements in order to avert any misunderstandings regarding things like how long the gig will last or how holidays and special events will affect your fee.

Although in some cases it may be appropriate or even necessary to waive your deposit, you should still make obtaining signed contracts part of your normal practice. If nothing else, they will be evidence that the engagement took place. Retain a copy of each contract and file it away after the job is done—you will need these at tax time.

Deposits

For the most part, the general public has become accustomed to the concept of deposits as a formality. A retail store will often require a deposit to hold merchandise. You expect to pay a deposit before moving into a house or an apartment, so why shouldn't *you* get one to secure your services?

Ask for a deposit of at least 20% to 30% of your fee, or for out-of-town engagements, at least 50%. Don't hesitate to enforce this rule; keep in mind that you are your own business agent and must look out for your own best interest.

You may request a nonrefundable deposit, which should be clearly stated on your contract. A nonrefundable deposit guarantees you some compensation for your time even when a client cancels, which is only fair as you may have turned down other offers to take that booking.

Bob's Story

One afternoon Bob received a phone call from a woman who wanted to hire his band for her wedding reception, which was due to take place about two months later. After a brief discussion, Bob and the young lady confirmed the band's availability, the time, the location, and the fee and agreed on a 20% deposit. The following day, they met to sign a contract and secure the deposit. Having done this, Bob put the date in his calendar.

About a month and a half later Bob received a phone call from the bride-to-be. With the reception only five days away, she informed him that the wedding was canceled and asked him to return her deposit. Somewhat stunned, he offered his condolences but quickly advised her that he couldn't give her a refund. This was the first time he'd had an engagement canceled and his deposit challenged. And, unfortunately, he hadn't included a nonrefundable-deposit clause in his contract. Bob had to stop and really give some thought to the situation. Was his decision fair? Was it deceptive?

Let's look at Bob's situation from a few different angles. First, when a date has been confirmed in someone's calendar and a deposit has been collected, that date is no longer available to other prospects, which means that Bob had to turn down any other engagements that fell on that date. Secondly, with most businesses, when a deposit has been collected and unique provisions made for the client, the deposit, or a portion of it, is usually retained. After discussing these issues, Bob was eventually able to convince his client of the income loss on his part because the date of the wedding had been turned down to another interested party.

Situations like Bob's happen all the time due to the lack of a simple clause. Make sure your client fully understands your policy on deposit returns. Your terms and stipulations should be clearly stated in writing. You can enforce this clause in several ways. You may require a thirty-day written notice of cancellation for a full or partial deposit refund. A contract may also stipulate that a deposit becomes non-refundable upon signing. The main purpose of a nonrefundable clause is to ensure a commitment from your client in an effort to stabilize dates on your calendar.

 *It's fine to be generous and forgiving enough to allow a client to exit a contractual agreement, but remember that your contract, with deposit and fee arrangements, are the very heart of your livelihood and should not be subject to the whims of an indecisive or noncommittal prospect.*

LEARN TO RECOGNIZE BUYING QUESTIONS

Are you available on weekends? Is your price negotiable? Do you play dance music? These are buying questions, which indicate that a prospect is definitely contemplating hiring you. Try to answer every question. Your prospect can't make a decision if you don't to answer her questions. If you're unable to address them all on the spot, assure her that you will get back to her soon. Make every effort to address unanswered questions no later than the next morning. The more time that passes, the greater the chances that your prospect will lose interest and seek out another band.

FOLLOW THROUGH AND CONFIRM

"I'll get back to you next week." This statement exemplifies a common evasion employed by unenthusiastic prospects. Here is where your employee/prospect relationship becomes sensitive. As your prospect teeters, trying to decide whether to become your client (or even remain a prospect), the likelihood of closing a deal will be diminished if you allow too much time to lapse.

Often that statement is nothing more than a brush-off. But in a lot of cases the prospect means just what he says—he's thinking about it and he plans to get back to you later. Perhaps live entertainment is to be discussed at his next manager's meeting, or maybe he has to get someone else's approval or coordinate schedules. These are all good reasons why you should follow through to confirm a possible engagement.

Most establishments operate on a low-risk or no-commitment basis: a low risk of losing money with no commitment to spend it. A good approach is to first "qualify" your prospect. When I say qualify, I mean find out early in the conversation whether he's truly interested and has a reasonable budget and resources to support live entertainment. Try to get a feel for what the establishment usually pays or is willing to pay. Simply ask a direct question, "Do you have a budget set aside for entertainment?"

and go from there. Listen closely to your prospect's reply. If there is no monetary figure mentioned, he is probably trying to feel *you* out. If you find yourself at a standstill and your prospect offers no suitable response, your next step is to state your minimum fee.

As with anything of a sales nature, if you don't qualify your prospect, you could find yourself wasting a lot of time. Don't oversell. If the prospect is genuinely interested, tie down the date, time, and price during your initial conversation or specify a time to do so shortly thereafter.

KNOW YOUR POSITION OF AUTHORITY

Take the initiative when someone calls and says that they want to hire you or your band for an engagement. Arrange to meet in order to tie down particulars, sign a contract, and obtain your deposit. Usually someone will ask the question, "How do I go about hiring your band?" This is good, because it puts you in a position of control. It's best to have a procedure or system by which you conduct business. Your prospect will respect the fact that you are organized and business minded. You're in the best position when you're in control. Place yourself in a position of authority. Get used to saying, "We require a 20% deposit upon signing a contract." Practice saying this until it comes naturally.

Sell your prospect on the idea that you are the authority on entertainment, not they. On occasion, you will encounter a prospect with a controlling nature. While it is true that they have power in the decision whether or not to hire you, you must stand your ground as someone of authority in your field. With a few successful experiences meeting and working with prospects, your confidence level will increase in a very short time. If your prospect decides not to hire you or your band, follow your meeting up with one of your professional, "personalized" post-cards. This will impress upon your prospect that you are a high-caliber businessperson.

Remember, good communication skills are a prime necessity with any business. The way you express your ideas and thoughts is a key factor in soliciting your musical talents and gaining the interest of potential clients. This basic rule will help you represent your band in the best possible light: always refer to your band in the plural (we, us, or our) rather than the singular (I, me, or my). Avoid referring to your band as if you were the only person involved, because a band is a group effort. (If you are a solo performer, obviously, the singular is appropriate.) The same concept applies when writing a letter, price quote, or bio.

A Few More Tips to Help Create Leverage and Authority

- A strong press kit should include a good song list with variety.

- Promotional items, such as posters, fliers, table tents, etc., will set you apart from everyone else.

- Use personal endorsements. After performing for some of the major clubs, corporations, and organizations in your area, ask the key person from each to write you a letter of recommendation. This can prove very effective in your press kit. An endorsement can influence a prospect's decision to hire you or your band. Make it a point to request one from every satisfied client.

- A good reputation is the single most important aspect that will affect the entire scope of your music career. Conduct yourself as professionally as possible and, at all cost, live up to your end of the bargain. Show up on time. Be personable and polite.

WHEN IT'S TIME TO MEET YOUR PROSPECT

If at all possible, arrange to meet your prospect on common ground, like at a restaurant, or even at the location of the engagement. Wherever you meet, you must sign a contract and collect a deposit. Try to set a meeting time that is convenient for your prospect. Better yet, let her pick the time and you pick the place. Choose a meeting place that you are comfortable with, and remember, it's easier to negotiate terms on your own turf.

Ask politely, "What's the best time for you to meet?" Try to make arrangements for the soonest possible day. At all cost, avoid letting your prospect put off meeting with you for more than a week. If your prospect has given you the runaround for more than a week, make no further attempts. It's highly likely that she is purposely avoiding you or just doesn't have the business tact to be up-front. Get to the point of your meeting quickly. Avoid engaging in drawn-out conversation. Find out all the necessary details concerning the engagement, sign your contract, and collect your deposit.

If a prospect has a busy work schedule that doesn't allow much flexibility during normal business hours, ask where she works and suggest meeting during lunch. Pick a location close to your prospect's place of work, because you want to eliminate possible excuses that will allow her to back out. If she is very busy and just can't decide on a definite date and location to meet with you, suggest a day when you'll be in the general neighborhood of her workplace. The key here is to close the deal as soon as possible after your prospect first shows an interest.

If you can afford it, insist on buying your prospect's lunch, making this known before your meeting. Don't view buying lunch as kissing up to a prospect but rather as leverage to make her feel a sense of obligation toward you. This tactic is more effective if you make the offer to pick up the tab before lunch and not after you've both eaten. (You can also write this off as a business expense at tax time.) Discourage your prospect from making last-minute arrangements. At some point it may become necessary to state that you must have a confirmation within a reasonable time period before the engagement. You may request that arrangements be finalized no later than four weeks ahead of time. People are sometimes lax about tying down details for an engagement that is several months away because they feel that they have plenty of time to deal with signing a contract and submitting a deposit. The same is true with returning a signed contract and a deposit by return mail, often leaving arrangements in limbo for an uncomfortable amount of time. Your objective is to finalize all arrangements within a two-week period.

The more time that passes before arrangements are confirmed, the greater are your chances of losing the prospect because a friend tells them about some other great band that they heard at Charlie's Bar the other night. Let your prospect know up front that you will need to sign a contract and receive a deposit before you can confirm a date on your calendar, and then ask him, "What's a convenient time for us to meet and tie down arrangements?" If your prospect replies, "Could you just send me a contract?" send it out as soon as possible, preferably the same day. Be sure to have a supply of NCR duplicate contract forms already printed up just for this purpose.

There are many factors that can delay a prospect in getting back with you to confirm a booking. Some people think that they will seem too anxious if they call a prospect after a long wait. In fact, your prospect may be too busy to get back to you at the previously appointed time. In that case, I say it's up to you to investigate. Don't feel embarrassed to make the first call. You are a businessperson with your own priorities and obligations. Go ahead and call your prospect and inform him that you are making contact to confirm arrangements for the date as previously discussed.

Because the date in question is drawing near, let your prospect know that someone else may be interested in that date and you want to give him first opportunity before you commit to someone else. This is a good tactic to use to find out exactly what your prospect intends to do. Often, you will be surprised to find out that your prospect was, in fact, just too busy or totally forgot to finalize arrangements with you. At any rate, you can now either make plans to sign a contract and obtain a deposit or find another prospect for that date.

MAINTAIN A PROFESSIONAL IMAGE OVER THE PHONE

Since it is highly impractical, and not always feasible, to network face-to-face, a good deal of your business will take place over the phone. The way you project your image over the phone is just as important as it is in a personal meeting. Be aware of your manner while you're on the phone; convey your professionalism at all times.

Imagine a nice, cozy home office with a personal computer, a fax machine, and a copier and to top it all off, a state-of-the-art digital answering machine. The outgoing message says, "Hello, you've reached Acme Entertainment. Please leave a message, or if you'd like to send a fax, press your start button after the beep." Now imagine that you come home one afternoon and your spouse yells from the other room, "Honey, there's a message for you on the answering machine." You spot the little red light flashing on your new digital answering machine, indicating that you may have a hot prospect who's eager to hire your band for any amount of money. You push the message button and a deep, authoritative voice says: "I'm interested in booking your band for our annual corporate party...." Quickly you dial the number, anxious for an answer. One ring...two rings...three rings, click! "Hello," the voice on the other end says, and before you can utter a single word, your 13-year-old screams, "Mama! Timmy didn't flush the toilet!" and now you're frozen with embarrassment. Of course, most people would be understanding about the situation, but nonetheless, you should make sure that phone calls with clients or prospects are uninterrupted from start to finish.

A TYPICAL PHONE-CALL SCENARIO

The following is a scenario typical of a phone call from a prospect, all of which will usually take place within the space of ten minutes. I have written this scenario with three different conclusions to reflect the three different responses a prospect is likely to give you after you've stated your fee. Before we begin, I'll cover some basics to consider when you take a prospect's call. First, the odds of a successful outcome are in your favor simply because the prospect called you, not the other way around. She may ask you an assortment of questions, like how many members are in your band, whether you have a singer, or whether you play dance music. Remember, your prospect can't make a decision if you can't answer her questions, especially if your band is not well established or has little or no following.

Always take notes during your phone conversations. If your prospect is not certain of a date, post a tentative date in your calendar until an exact date can be confirmed. Gather all the information you can before quoting your price. Giving a price quote before you obtain all the necessary information may create confusion or negative results. It's best to state your deposit requirements at the same time that you quote your fee: "Our minimum fee is $600 with a 20% deposit." If your prospect tells you that your fee is out of her price range, don't discontinue the conversation and hang up. Instead, ask what the budget for that particular event is, listen to her answer, and proceed. At that point, it's up to you to accept or decline. The unique advantage of this scenario is that you are in the position of control.

A Typical Phone Call
Might Go Like This:

Caller: Hello, I'm Jane Smith. I saw you perform about two months ago and I would like to know if you're available for a function our company is planning in October. And how much do you charge?

You: *I appreciate you considering me. Could you hold just a moment, while I get my appointment book?...Hello, Ms. Smith. Now, what is the date, and what type of function is it?*

Caller: The date is October 5th. It's a grand opening for our new store location.

You: *Is it in town?*

Caller: Yes, the location is 3248 N. Rockwell.

You: *What are the start and finish times?*

Caller: It starts at 7:00 P.M. an goes until 10:00 P.M.

You: *My fee is.... [State your minimum fee, or a higher figure if you feel your prospect will accept it, followed by your deposit requirements.]*

Conclusion #1

Caller: That sounds reasonable, could you send me a contract?

You: *I'll send a contract out this week. Let me make sure that I have all the correct information. That's October 5th from 7:00 P.M. to 10:00 P.M. at 3248 N. Rockwell, and it's a grand opening for your new store. Is that correct?*

Caller: Yes.

You: *Is there a phone number where I can reach you?*

Caller: Yes, it's 555-1234, or you can page me at 555-5678.

You: *What is your mailing address?*

Caller: 1502 W. Be There Street

You: *Okay, and what's the proper spelling of your name?*

Caller: That's J-A-N-E S-M-I-T-H.

You: *Thank very much Ms. smith, I will have a contract in the mail shortly, and as soon as I get that back from you I'll confirm your event in my calendar. [Of course, your conversation doesn't have to be this calculated. Just relax, don't hurry, and don't act overly eager.]*

Conclusion #2

Caller: That's quite a bit higher than what we had intended to pay.

You: *What is your budget for this particular engagement?*

Caller: $X is all we have set aside for entertainment.

You: *Okay, I can work with that price. [Proceed to obtain remaining information and finalize arrangements.]*

Conclusion #3

> **Caller:** That's quite a bit higher than what we had intended to pay.
> **You:** *What is your budget for this particular engagement?*
> **Caller:** *$X* is all we have set aside for entertainment.
> **You:** *I'm sorry, I can't work with that price, but thank you very much for considering me, and please call again.*

STAY IN TOUCH WITH FORMER CLIENTS

A prospect or client may contact you about an engagement that you can't commit to because of a previous booking. In such an event, make every effort to assist in locating another band. Your willingness to assist builds trust and confidence from your prospect or former client that could help develop a long-lasting professional relationship.

Making your living as a musician depends heavily on maintaining your former clients' trust and loyalty. Clearly, private engagements will yield greater income opportunities than club and restaurant gigs. The challenge is gaining repeat bookings through former clients who trust and admire your band. To help ensure client trust and loyalty, you must maintain periodic communication in the form of follow-up calls, postcards, mailings, etc. Any means that keeps your band's name on a former client's mind will pay off in the long run.

After you have performed at a private function, whether for a corporation or an individual, make contact a few days after the engagement, preferably with a follow-up postcard. A personally designed card is always more effective than the generic type when you want to make a lasting impression. If you can afford it, have at least two styles printed, one to send after an initial meeting, regardless of whether a prospect accepts or declines to hire you, and another to send after the engagement. Don't consider this a waste of time and postage. A postcard demonstrates that you are a reliable businessperson and makes your band stand out for possible consideration in the future. Although it's convenient to just stick a label on the back of a card, something as simple as a handwritten address can project sincerity rather than a distant, impersonal image.

Make the most of former-client relationships. Staying in touch two to three times a year keeps you or your band fresh in people's minds and increases your chance of being considered for upcoming events. In a way, you're creating a customer-service relationship that your client will trust and appreciate. Inform former clients if you change your phone number or address so they can update their personal files.

SOME FACTS ABOUT FAXING

A fax machine can be a very important and useful tool when it comes to marketing yourself and your band. Not only is it convenient to fax a press release to notify local entertainment publications of your band's performance schedule, but you can also use the fax machine to help generate new performance opportunities.

At times you must be aggressive in your pursuit of work. When business is slow, start faxing your press kit along with your current performance schedule to clubs and restaurants that you have not previously contacted. (You can use the *Gig-O-Rama* software to set up an extensive "Clubs and Restaurants" database specifically for this purpose.) Before faxing, make a brief inquiry call to find out the name of the manager or person in charge of hiring entertainment so you can target your fax to a specific department or individual. You may be surprised at the number of callbacks you receive.

Make a follow-up call the next day to those who do not respond to your fax. When you finally make contact, simply state, "I'm following up to make sure that you received the fax I sent yesterday." Your key person may respond in one of six ways: (1) "I did receive your fax, but right now we already have a band that we are very pleased with." (2) "We don't usually have live entertainment, but I'll keep your information on file for special engagements in the future." (3) "We work through a booking agency." (4) "I would like to speak with you—could you stop in later this week?" (5) We've tried live entertainment in the past, but it didn't work out for us." (6) "We don't have a budget for entertainment."

Be prepared to hear a multitude of excuses why entertainment won't work for some establishments. Go back over the list of responses and think about how you could persuade each individual to think differently.

Negotiation means working out an agreement by trying to reach a compromise. Managers and agents are, in essence, professional negotiators. Their expertise lies in their ability to recognize the negotiable factors of music industry–related affairs.

Some bands and musicians may have difficulty making wise business deals or stumble in the negotiation process. No matter what your band's level of notoriety is, avoid allowing your client or prospect to lay down the ground rules. When your prospect asks you a buying question, recognize that *you* have the upper hand. When you have the opportunity to state your price and terms, it's important to know what's negotiable and when to negotiate. I'm not saying that every contract you sign must become a complex chess game as you alter each clause listed, but view the negotiation process as a "user friendly" option for your prospect or client. For instance, after you've stated your minimum fee and your prospect has informed you that he has a limited budget of *x* dollars, would you just say "Sorry, maybe next time"? I didn't think so. If his budget is not too far below your minimum fee and you feel that your band can still profit from it, negotiate!

If your prospect just *has* to have *your* band for that special party, you have extreme bargaining power. Think about how your terms can be negotiated in order to accommodate your prospect's small budget. The first thing you might consider is time. Instead of the three hours your prospect asked you to play, offer two hours. If the engagement is two months from now on a Friday or Saturday night, and you want to reserve your weekend nights for higher-paying gigs, ask if they would switch to a weeknight. There are plenty of options if you give it enough thought. Making a satisfactory arrangement is not difficult if you know what, and when, to negotiate.

Establish terms that you or your band are willing to work with. For example, know just where to draw the line if you choose to render your services for less than your minimum fee or to perform for more than your maximum number of hours, and decide how many charity functions to participate in this year. These general guidelines will help you negotiate profitably and effectively.

PRESENTING YOUR CONTRACT TO A CLIENT

A contract by any other name is still a contract. A musician friend once told me that some of his clients don't like to sign contracts but they *will* sign a "letter of agreement." In essence, they're nothing more than pieces of paper with a few carefully chosen words. However, there is much to consider before your client-to-be signs on the dotted line. First realize that both a contract and letter-of-agreement are legally binding documents that spell out mutually agreed terms between two parties.

Although a contract and a letter of agreement function in the same capacity, the primary difference between the two is the language or terminology that each document employs. A contract can be as brief as one page or as long as thirty, or even more, depending on the complexities of the negotiated terms. For a local musician/performing artist, a general entertainment contract will rarely exceed one page. Look at the examples on pages 69 and 70.

A letter of agreement is simply what it states it is: a single-page document written in letter form. Its language is simple and uncomplicated, like that of a common letter—see the example on page 71. It is strictly up to the individual which one to use.

Occasionally, an establishment that regularly employs entertainers will provide its own contract or letter of agreement, which is fine in most cases. If you or your band is ever presented with a contract, read it carefully and question any clauses that are not clear or seem not to be in your favor. Never feel embarrassed to ask questions before signing a contract. I would feel more comfortable asking about an unclear clause *before* an incident occurred than dealing with it afterward.

SAMPLE SHORT-TERM CONTRACT

THIS CONTRACT, for personal services of performer(s) on the engagement described below, made this_____day of _____,19____, between the undersigned purchaser (herein called PURCHASER) and_____ performer(s). The performers are engaged severally on the terms and conditions on the face hereof.

I represent that the performer(s) already designated have agreed to be bound by said terms and conditions. The performers severally agree to render services under the undersigned leader.

RIGHT TO SUBCONTRACT: Band / Performer (s) reserve the right to fulfill their contractual obligations by contracting with additional parties including but not limited to substitute performers.

1. Name and Location of Engagement_____

2. Name of Band or Performer_____

3. Date(s), Starting and Finishing time _____ — ___ : _____ to ___ : _____

4. Type of Engagement (specify whether dance, stage show, banquet etc.) _____

5. Wage Agreed Upon $_____. This wage includes expenses agreed by the employer in accordance with attached schedule, or a schedule to be furnished to the PURCHASER on or before the date of engagement.

PURCHASER will make payments as follows: A ____% deposit in the amount of, $_____ is due upon signing of contract, by Cash, Check or Money Order, payable to the undersigned representative. The remaining balance of $_____will be due on, or before date of engagement. All deposits are nonrefundable regardless of cancellation by contractor.

PURCHASER   REPRESENTATIVE OF PERFORMERS

_____   _____
signature   signature

SAMPLE LONG-TERM CONTRACT

Starting Date: _____/_____year_____

Ending Date: _____/_____year_____

THIS CONTRACT, for personal services of performer(s) at the engagement described below, is made this_____day of _____,19____, between the undersigned Purchaser (herein called PURCHASER) and_____ performer(s). The performers are engaged severally under the terms and conditions on the face hereof. I represent that the performer(s) already designated have agreed to be bound by said terms and conditions. The performers severally agree to render services under the undersigned leader.

RIGHT TO SUBCONTRACT: Performer (s) reserves the right to fulfill these contractual obligations by contracting with additional parties including but not limited to substitute performers.

PROMOTION AND ADVERTISING PROVISIONS: Under the exclusive provisions of this contract, PURCHASER agrees to include Performer(s) in all advertising and promotional efforts currently utilized by PURCHASER, to include some or all of the following: radio, TV, newspaper, magazine, marquee display (throughout the duration of contract), table tents, fliers, etc. It is further agreed that the PURCHASER will put forth a conscious and willing effort to abide by all of the aforementioned terms.

SECONDARY EVENTS: The term, SECONDARY EVENTS applies to any special event that PURCHASER/ ESTABLISHMENT engages in, outside of normal business activities, such as: WEDDING RECEPTIONS, CORPORATE PARTIES, HOLIDAYS and HOLIDAY EVENTS, or any other SOCIAL OR PRIVATE FUNCTIONS hosted by the undersigned PURCHASER. Entertainment services included with the above mentioned activities will be at a rate of $_____ for the evening, SEPARATE AND APART from ESTABLISHMENT'S usual activities.

1. Name of Establishment_____

2. Name of Band or Performer_____

3. Day(s) each week_____
   Starting and Finishing time ____ : ____ to ____ : ____

4. Type of Engagement (specify dance, stage show, banquet, etc.)
   _____

5. PURCHASER agrees to pay a weekly wage of $_____ in the form of cash or a check made payable to the undersigned representative on the last performance night of each week.

_____   _____
PURCHASER   REPRESENTATIVE

SAMPLE LETTER OF AGREEMENT

This is to confirm that I, Maurice Johnson, agree to perform on Friday, May 14, 1999, from 7:00 P.M. until 9:00 P.M., for the West Side Social Club. In return, the West Side Social Club agrees to pay a fee of $300.00, which will require an initial 20% deposit of $60.00 upon the signing of this agreement. The remaining balance of $240.00 will be paid on or before the evening of the engagement.

_____   _____

Purchaser   Date

_____   _____

Performer   Date

To eliminate confusion or to keep a prospect from dragging her feet about signing a contract and sending your deposit, try this! Along with a self-addressed, postage-paid envelope, include a cover letter that reads something like the following example.

Dear Ms. Jacobs:

Thank you for selecting *[you or your band's name]* for your upcoming event. I look forward to entertaining your guests. When you have a moment please fill out the enclosed contract and return the white copy along with your deposit check. I am anxious to confirm your event in our calendar as soon as possible. If you have any questions about our arrangements, feel free to contact me at (555) 123-1234.

Sincerely,

Maurice Johnson
The Jazz Guitar of Maurice Johnson

A letter like this may sound a bit stuffy, but it's very effective for confirming a booking and collecting your deposit in a polite but direct manner. Remember to have your contracts printed on NCR (no carbon required) forms in duplicate.

SOME IMPORTANT FACTS ABOUT CONTRACTS

- A contract does not become legally binding until both parties sign.

- A contract must have mutuality and consideration of both parties, meaning that both sides must agree to the terms of the contract.

- If you must fax a contract for the second party to sign, let it serve only to confirm a mutual agreement. *It does not replace the original document.* Somewhere in the faxed document, include the following statement: "The original contract will follow in confirmation hereof by mail." Mail a hard copy for the second party to sign and keep a copy for your records.

- Keep all contracts and faxed documents in a secure file for at least one year after the date signed.

- Any document on fax paper can fade to an almost indistinguishable state in a matter of weeks. Be sure to make photocopies of all of your important faxed documents.

- Both signing parties must have mutual authority to do so or the contract may be invalid. Make sure a responsible, authorized person signs your contract.

Check It Out! ▶ *Certain formalities will apply to almost any trade or profession. Your career as a working musician is no different. Routine activities, such as filing copyrights, negotiating contracts, and other official acts, can be viewed as the glue that holds a working musician's career together.*

WHAT DID WE LEARN?

- Your prospect or client will most likely also be your key person.

- Your relationship with your key person must always be mutually pleasant and professional.

- The first rule when booking a private engagement is to get a signed contract.

- The second rule when booking an engagement is to collect a deposit.

- Sell your prospect on the idea that you are the authority on entertainment, not they.

- To "qualify" your prospect means to find out early in the conversation if he or she is truly interested and has a reasonable budget to support live entertainment.

- When setting a time to meet with a prospect interested in hiring your band, the sooner the better.

- If prospects don't get back to you when they said they would, call and inform them that you need to confirm arrangements.

- Date, price, and payment arrangements are all negotiable terms in your contract.

CHAPTER 6

When You Perform

I 'll admit that I still get the nervous jitters when driving to a gig or during sound check, and sometimes just before the first set begins. As soon as the music starts, the tension usually disappears. However, if I'm not careful my anxiety could reveal itself through quickened speech and lots of sweating as I try to relate to a lifeless and unresponsive audience between songs. Believe me, it can be a bone-chilling experience to feel yourself transform from a cool musician to a guitar-wielding Barney Fife.

WHAT MAKES *YOU* SO SPECIAL?

When employed correctly, your own uniqueness can bring you greater money-making potential as a musician. To be unique simply means to possess any physical or personal attribute unlike others'—it could be size, shape, volume, height, sound, taste, weight, endurance, beauty, or a host of other things. What is it that makes you like one band's sound more than another's, or even like a particular brand of toothpaste? Our entire world trade system depends on what products or services are preferred over others. Manufacturers spend billions of dollars each year on advertising, just to prove that their goods or services are unique among their competitors'.

Uniqueness can make the difference between success and failure. Look at how entertainers over the years have exploited their individuality and made money because of it. Elvis Presley's musical style and gyrating hips stimulated much controversy in the media and even among heads of state, but his undeniable uniqueness evoked the multimillion-dollar Elvis-mania that shows no sign of subsiding, even almost three decades after his death. There are countless other success stories of bands and entertainers capitalizing on their uniqueness, even though uniqueness doesn't always equate to profound talent. (The days of fantastic, pyrotechnic light and smoke shows come to mind, when musicians would paint themselves from head to toe and bite off the heads of snakes, all to the sound of screaming guitars driven through a mountain of speakers.)

What makes *you* so unique? You'll have to find the answer that question and demonstrate it if you hope to gain more than mediocre success in the music industry. You have probably heard the expression, "There's nothing new under the sun." It's safe to say that everyone has borrowed something from someone else at one time or another. The fact is that everybody's point of inspiration originates from some external influence.

Check It Out! ▶ *Learn from other performers' examples as you develop your own style. Incorporate what you have learned into your act until it comes natural. This process will occur over and over as you pick characteristics of your favorite performers that ultimately merge to create your unique signature.*

GIG ETIQUETTE

By all means, be sociable at your gigs. Don't hide or make yourself unavailable to your audience when you're on a break. As a working musician, you're always in the public eye whether you like it or not. You must continue to sell yourself—it's called *public appeal*. Your demeanor during breaks is just as important as your actual stage performance.

Be on Time

When you go for a job interview, you show up on time—or better yet, you get there a little early. Well, the same thing applies to gigging. Your reputation is at stake every time your band performs, so defend it with all you've got.

The worst thing you can do as a newcomer is develop bad habits. Honest mistakes are one thing, but plain old bad habits are unacceptable. They can set you up for a short-lived music career. Constantly showing up late, getting drunk on the gig, or always needing a ride can spell certain death as you become some club owner's or band leader's worst nightmare or last resort. No one likes to hire, or even be around, an undependable musician. Treat your music career with the utmost respect.

Don't Practice at a Gig

Never rehearse on stage in front of an audience. I can't emphasize this enough. Going over changes before a song or stopping in the middle and starting over is very unprofessional. Avoid discussing song arrangements while on stage, especially within earshot of your audience. Your rehearsals should take place away from the public eye. Band members discussing song arrangements while on stage is a pretty good sign that you're not rehearsing enough.

Alcohol, Drugs, and the Performing Musician

Too much of anything is a bad thing. Frequent visits to the bar during your band's break time can become cause for concern when your guitar player's "Mr. Hyde" personality emerges during the third set of your gig. I pondered for a long time whether to include this topic, but unfortunately I have to concede that this problem is all too real subject for musicians and other performing artists at every level. The performing artist who fights the destructive effects of alcohol or substance abuse will eventually have to face the problem head-on, hopefully not at the expense of his career. Such a bout can be particularly blinding for a person who is in denial of his own desperate situation.

Mike was one of the greatest singers I have ever had the privilege of performing with. Sadly, years of alcohol abuse rendered him almost completely dysfunctional as a professional. A primary symptom of this was his chronic tendency to arrive late to gigs—anywhere from 45 minutes to an hour and a half late. As talented a musician as Mike was, his chances for a promising music career spiraled into a virtually unrecoverable state.

STAGE PRESENCE

Be conscious of your stage presence and showmanship, but don't preoccupy yourself with trying to project an image that's not really you. Audiences want to be entertained, but never feel that you have to put on a floor show to satisfy them. Just relax and be yourself. Some performers seem to have a knack for entertaining an audience with natural showmanship and keeping their attention throughout the evening. A good showman is not necessarily a great musician, but if not, is able to divert attention from her lack of musical ability. A musician who interacts well or flashes an occasional smile at an audience will shine through every time.

You can learn a lot by watching how other performers work with an audience. I know a woman who has performed a piano-bar act for many years, and she also happens to be a former beauty-pageant winner. Her personality is such that she has won the hearts of a loyal following that attends almost all of her shows. Her charismatic appeal draws attention wherever she goes. Carol has taken her act far beyond the typical piano-bar lounge routine of performing a few standards for an audience of nocturnal conversationalists. When Carol sits down at the piano, all those around her give their undivided attention. Her flamboyant antics and dramatic entrances make her audience eager for a night of entertainment and fun. I have had the good fortune to perform happy-hour sets, on certain nights of the week, just before Carol came on.

One evening as I was winding up my last set, she casually strolled into the bar dressed as Mae West. She really played up the role and immediately captured her audience. But that's not all—she was so clever in her ability to capture her audience and create a memorable event for everyone that she even brought a camera and had audience members pose with her for snapshots. (In fact, I have a photograph around here somewhere of myself posing with Mae West.)

Observing charismatic performers like this can teach you and inspire you to come up with your own ways to captivate your audience.

MAKE EVERY PERFORMANCE YOUR BEST PERFORMANCE

Entertaining doesn't have to mean being funny or becoming a comedian on stage. But however you do it, your ability to captivate an audience can prove invaluable, especially when there is a potential client in your audience. Start viewing every audience member as a prospect. Don't be selective or judgmental during a performance or social interaction with your audience, because you never know who's considering employing your services.

The pressure of having to learn all the latest tunes by a variety of artists in hopes of satisfying the whole audience is tough. You will come to realize that you can't please everybody all the time. I've seen bandleaders worry and sweat at break time over whether every member of the audience is satisfied. You can't do it, it's impossible, so don't even try it. You must be confident in and comfortable with what *you* do and know that you're performing your best.

HOLDING ON TO YOUR AUDIENCE

The best technique for holding an audience's attention is simple interaction and developing a personal bond. This requires real people skills. You must be genuine, sincere, and unpretentious when relating to an audience. Be assertive and make an earnest effort to gain the trust and faith of your audience. During your breaks go out among them and introduce yourself. Shake hands and make conversation. This technique works well in small rooms and clubs. Get to know regulars on a first-name basis. This is also a good way to develop a following. Captivating an audience with your personality and charm helps to encourage a reciprocal response from them.

One Night at the Club

I remember one night in particular when I had two gigs booked for the same night. My first gig that evening was at a bookstore/coffee shop playing solo jazz guitar from 6:30 to 8:30 . The second was an 8:00 club gig with my trio. I had made arrangements for the band to play a laid-back first set without me. With two activities in one night, I was pretty hyper, realizing that after the bookstore gig I would have to immediately tear down my gear and drive to the club some three miles away. When I got there the club was about one-third full. Needless to say, my adrenaline was running pretty high. After giving a visual cue to the band from across the room, I quickly rushed up to the microphone and announced, "We're the Maurice Johnson trio, how about a round of applause for two of the world's finest musicians! We're going to take a short break, so please stay with us."

My first objective was to regain my composure, and then I had to maintain the interest of a Friday-night crowd. After my announcement, I immediately went out into the audience and introduced myself to each and every one of them. By personally interacting with the audience I planted a sense of curiosity with each audience member. Those who didn't leave the club during the break probably felt an obligation not to walk out in the middle of a song once the band started playing again.

Introducing yourself and making enough eye contact while on stage sends out a signal that suggests, "Don't leave just yet, or I'll be insulted." Your relationship with your audience is of the utmost importance throughout the evening. If it makes you feel more comfortable, pretend the audience is in your living room. As you and your band experience more actual performances, your ability to communicate with and read an audience will improve.

BREAK TIME: HOW LONG IS TOO LONG?

Generally your breaks should last about 15 minutes, unless otherwise specified by the person or establishment that hired you. I have seen some bands take up to 30 minutes, which, in my opinion, is too long. For a house band in a typical club, a 30-minute break can make the audience restless—it's not cool when a member of the audience has to ask when will you start playing again. A break longer than half an hour can create an even less desirable result, as some audience members leave the establishment with a few derogatory comments about your band's unprofessional behavior. This casts a bad reflection on the establishment, as well. Lengthy breaks are typical of inexperienced bands and are looked upon unfavorably. Always be aware of your audience and conscious of time passing during your breaks.

A musician friend (I'll call him "Joe") shared this story with me during a brief discussion about just how long a break should be. Joe was acquainted with an up-and-coming local band and, like many of us, often tries to assist in a new band's success. Enterprising musician that he is, Joe had a good friend who worked for a Nashville record label as a talent scout. This talent-scout friend was in town for the weekend to check out some of the local acts, so Joe, determined to have his friend hear this fledgling band, personally drove him to the club where they were playing. When they arrived, the band was taking a break. No big deal, Joe thought. After ordering a couple of drinks, Joe walked over to say hello to the band and ask when they would start playing again, not telling them who was in the audience for fear of making the guys nervous. By then, our talent scout was working on his second drink, eager to hear the young band.

Half an hour later, he was getting more impatient with each passing minute, as the band continued to break. Before long, he said, "I can't use this band, they're too unprofessional. Let's go someplace else." Joe was disappointed and never had the heart to tell the band that they had missed out on a rare opportunity.

DOS AND DON'TS THAT AFFECT YOUR AUDIENCE

- Don't turn your back to your audience while performing. Even though some respected musicians (such as legendary jazz trumpeter Miles Davis) have performed this way, this may be viewed as insulting or disrespectful.

- Interact with your audience regularly throughout the evening; don't ignore them.

- Pick out a member of your audience and occasionally relate to that individual verbally or visually.

- Don't act too serious—your audience wants to be entertained, not depressed.

- Smile...a lot!

- Don't complain to your audience.

- Whatever you do, don't chastise an audience member for not appreciating your music.

WORKING WITH CLUB OWNERS

Every club owner is different. A successful club owner will rarely relate to you beyond your capacity as a professional, hired musician. On the other hand, a less experienced club owner might confide in you, sometimes relying on your experience and feel for the local music scene. If you or your band is ever in such a situation, play it up. Offer suggestions and make the club owner feel that you are interested in helping his establishment. This is in your best interest, too, because a bad reflection on the club can be a bad reflection on you, and vice versa. A club owner will appreciate your suggestions and value your advice.

This type of rapport with an owner can give you an advantage over other local bands and musicians and can also give the owner a sense of loyalty toward you. You will likely be his first choice to perform for special engagements or for other considerations. This doesn't necessarily mean above-average pay, but a solid relationship with a good club owner can help float you and your band during slower times.

LONG-TERM ENGAGEMENTS

Don't let a club owner think that she can expect to have you and your services exclusively, lock, stock, and barrel. Make her aware that on occasion an alternate engagement may arise, in which case you will assist in finding a substitute. Inform the owner of any previous obligations before committing to a long-term agreement. Prepare a schedule of your upcoming engagements to show when you will be absent, and ask if you can post it on the office bulletin board to help avoid misunderstandings or conflicts when you're not present.

Sometimes a club owner will expect you to assume full responsibility for finding and paying substitute musicians when you have to miss a regular gig. With this arrangement, transactions between you and the club owner can continue without interruption: the owner pays you as if you performed on the evening of your absence, and then you just have to duke it out with the substitute. You may choose to offer the sub a portion of your pay instead of all of it, so by all means, don't reveal the original pay scale to your sub. Be sure to keep a record of payments you make to subs.

Once you have negotiated a comfortable salary with a club or restaurant, slow down on booking outside gigs beyond already existing commitments. A club owner will not tolerate a musician who is too busy to fulfill a contractual obligation. A preoccupation with overlapping bookings can spell sudden death to your dream gig.

A regular gig, even if it doesn't pay very much, does have its advantages:

- It puts you before the public frequently, increasing the likelihood of an occasional pickup gig.

- It keeps you active.

- You can view it as getting paid to practice your performance technique.

- It offers you a stable base from which to build a regular audience.

- It helps enhance the club's image, which may in turn enhance yours.

- It provides an opportunity for you to invite a prospect or booking agent to see and hear you in action, in an actual working environment.

- You can start a mailing list by having audience members sign a guest book.

- It helps your band develop the ability to read an audience—for example, learning to call appropriate songs to fit the mood.

BE RESPONSIBLE FOR YOUR OWN EQUIPMENT

Never assume that other musicians will let you use their equipment. Guitarists, be sure to have your own cords. Drummers, provide your own cymbals and sticks. I suggest that each band member have his or her own gig bag to keep a supply of necessary items, such as cords, batteries, guitar strings, drumsticks, tuners, etc.

Sometimes certain equipment, perhaps drums, amps, or a piano, will be furnished for a gig. Make sure that all arrangements regarding borrowed gear are confirmed before the performance date. These terms should be stated in your contract or an attached rider.

Each year, as eagerly anticipated, warm, sunny days sketch a rainbow of color over a once frostbitten landscape, man's rambunctious spirit is reawakened. Break out the tents, sailboats, and golf clubs—it's summertime! Warm weather and outdoor engagements can be fun and entertaining for everyone involved. However, in contrast to the relative stability of an indoor venue, outdoor gigs pose the threat of unforeseen quirks of nature. A gust of wind or sudden shower could prove detrimental to instruments and equipment. For your own good, be sure to take extra precautions when booking outdoor engagements. Your clients are concerned with entertaining guests and having a good time, and they typically have little or no regard for the safety of your band's hard-earned equipment. When you're negotiating an outdoor engagement, ask your prospective client if there is an alternate location to be used in the event of rain or other adverse weather conditions.

A Few Tips for Outdoor Engagements

- Ask your prospect to have you play under an awning.

- Avoid setting up on a poolside, especially if there are swimmers.

- Avoid setting up in direct sunlight with no shade.

- Ask to be placed away from high-traffic areas, and if your band is performing in a ground-level, open area, ask your client to rope off the back and sides of the performance space. Never allow guests to walk through your performance area, between equipment, etc.

- Supervise the stage and performance area during breaks. Never leave the area unattended.

- If wind is a threat, place instruments in their cases during breaks.

- Provide your own 50- to 100-foot, grounded and shielded AC power cord and six-way, surge-protected power strips.

The time has finally come when your band is hired to open for that national recording band the Big National Act—which happens to be your favorite band. You and your band have waited a long time for this moment and your nerves are on edge from fear and excitement. The promoter who's bringing them to town wants your band to open because you sound a lot like the Big National Act and are sure to knock the socks off of ticket buyers. I'm sure this scenario strikes a familiar chord with some of you: you're tempted to perform one of your heroes' songs to flatter or impress them, but that is the worst thing you could do as an opening act. It could blow your chances of networking with the Big National Act, because they may be insulted by an opening act that sounds too much like them or seems to be trying to imitate them. This can be a problem when inexperienced promoters try to match the opening act with the headliner in terms of musical style.

In any case, it is always a good idea to learn something about the band you are opening for, and make sure your band's song selections are well thought out.

 A big concert gig provides you an excellent opportunity to network on a much higher level than usual. The common expression is, "It's not what you know but who you know;" I call it "success by association."

BEHIND THE SCENES

A lot more goes on behind the scenes at a concert than most starry-eyed fans realize. Preconcert preparation resembles an ant farm, as the headlining act's sound and stage crew scurries about, hurriedly setting up for the evening's event. As a first timer, your natural inclination will be to stay out of the way until they're finished and hope that there's enough room left on stage for your band to set up. It is indeed best to allow the stage crew to complete their work without interruption. It can be intimidating to know that your band will have to set up somewhere in the middle of the main act's jungle of speakers, amps, mics, cords, and monitors. On a positive note, there will be a stage manager, who is responsible for seeing that your band's setup goes smoothly.

When you and your band arrive, locate the promoter or individual who hired you and ask him to introduce you to the stage manager. You will need to make sure that person knows how many mics your band is going to need. For a concert performance, your drums and amps will be miked and run through the sound system, so be certain to include these in the number of mics you request. And relax—stage crews are aware of the uncertainty an opening act can feel.

THE EMCEE

No concert performance is complete without a grand introduction by an emcee (from M.C., or master of ceremonies). The emcee will usually be a popular radio disc jockey or other high-profile individual. His or her job is to introduce each performing act to the audience. Unless, of course, you're band needs no introduction, or you're the hardest-working band in show business, the emcee can add that needed twinge of color and excitement to lead into your performance. The emcee will likely get information from your press kit to share with your audience. Often the emcee will ask you for last-minute details, such as the correct pronunciation of your name or when and where your CD will be available. If an emcee is going to speak on your band's behalf, make sure they have something worthwhile to say. If there is something in particular you'd like the audience to know, inform the emcee in plenty of time before your band goes on.

THE STAGE PLOT

As your band spends more time performing together, you will find that each member has a particular spot on stage that he or she either prefers or necessity dictates. You may also have an alternate setup that your band sometimes uses, depending on the size and layout of the stage or performance area. To help things run smoothly when your band is preparing for a concert or stage show, make a drawing, or *stage plot,* of the stage layout your band prefers and include it in your press kit. Use simple squares and circles to indicate amps, drums, main speakers, monitors, and so on. Your stage plot will be a great help to the stage and sound crew as they prepare the stage for your band's performance. You can avoid wasting valuable time before sound check trying to figure where each band member will stand during a performance.

Sound check is just as important as your actual performance. The objective of a sound check is to get the best possible mix and balance between instruments and microphones, tailored to the room or environment you will perform in. Each room, stage, club, or outdoor area has unique acoustic properties that greatly affect the quality of your band's sound output. Your goal is to get a sound you're happy with during sound check so you can keep tweaking, tuning, and other adjustments to a minimum during your actual performance.

Here are some routine checkpoints and general maintenance tips. They should become part of your band's normal operation.

- Make sure all band members tune up before every gig. There are many tuners on the market that allow you to tune accurately with your volume completely off.

- Your band should share a gig bag that contains a supply of extra quarter-inch cables, three-prong extension cords, power-supply strips, wire cutters, duct tape, and electrical tape.

- Keep up with faulty guitar and speaker cables, equipment power-supply cords, and adapters. Either repair them or replace them quickly. Don't procrastinate or wait until the band is stopped dead in its tracks during a performance because somebody didn't replace a $10 cable.

The ideal time to do a sound check is just after you set up your equipment, in the absence of an audience. Understandably, this is sometimes not possible, depending on time constraints beyond your control or the actual performance environment. Whenever possible, when your band is booked for a concert or stage performance, request at least a half hour for a sound check.

- Discussing song arrangements while on stage is a good indication that your band is not rehearsing enough

- Observe other performers to learn how they hold their audiences' attention.

- Don't hide or make yourself unavailable while you're on break.

- Generally your breaks should last about 15 minutes, unless otherwise specified by the person or establishment that hired you.

- Your demeanor during breaks is just as important as your actual stage performance.

- Club owners will not tolerate a musician who is too busy to fulfill a contractual obligation.

- Prepare a stage plot for concert performances, and be sure you get time to run a sound check.

CHAPTER 7

Making Money from Your Music

"So, how do I find gigs?!" That's a fair question, and the first thing I have to say is, "The answer is persistence." No book can guarantee you a single gig. I can only assure you that your chances of emerging victoriously are greatly increased by simply being aware and applying some of the suggestions offered here. Ultimately your success depends solely on the degree of effort you put into pursuing gigs. You may not realize it yet, but your creativity doesn't end with just music. If you intend to become a full-time musician/performing artist, be prepared and willing to explore a variety of options that will exploit all of your existing abilities.

PREPARING FOR THE WEEKS AHEAD

This is a common occurrence: someone goes out and buys a harmonica, rips open the box, throws the instructions aside, and says, "I'll learn as I go." And you know what? They most likely will. So I encourage you to go right ahead, roll up your sleeves and jump in. I am aware that some of you aren't quite sure how or even where to begin. The following is a systematic approach to the fundamental steps of organizing a database along with basic strategies for those stepping out for the first time. To make it easier, I've broken this section up into a five-week schedule. Those of you with some experience may want to glance over this as a refresher to help sharpen your skills, or else you can advance directly to "Where to Find the Work" on page 93. In order to take full advantage of the allotted time, prepare before you get started. Give yourself a chance to absorb the information thoroughly. If you need to spend more than one week on a particular phase, do so without procrastinating.

Week 1: Explore

Get started by reviewing the selection of possible gigs listed in "Where to Find the Work," below. You'll have to do some research and take detailed notes of addresses, phone numbers, fax numbers, e-mail addresses, etc. as you explore possible gigs in your area. I suggest that you obtain a notebook specifically for this purpose. At this phase it is important to use all your resources. To enhance your efforts, ask friends and other active musicians for possible leads.

Don't take for granted that any establishment or organization that doesn't currently book live entertainment would not be interested in the idea. Consider it an achievement if you successfully convince a business to try live music for the first time. Some small establishments may welcome the idea of hiring your band on a trial basis. For you first-timers, this is the experience you're after.

Week 2:
Organize Your Database

This week should be spent setting up your database. If you own a computer, transfer all of the information in your written list to a database program. (There is a "Clubs and Restaurants" database already set up in the *Gig-O-Rama* software.) This will become the heart of your personal database and prove invaluable as a constant reference. Keep it updated with any new information you get. Use the "Comments" field and update it each time you contact someone. This way you can keep an accurate log that documents the specific details of each conversation. If you don't own a computer just yet, you should strongly consider employing this single most powerful technological marvel of the 20th century as a practical and invaluable aid. You might ask, "What would I do with a computer?" Look around you! Since the advent of the personal computer, access to information on just about any subject has accelerated at an incredible rate. Today, life and technology are moving at a very fast pace. If you stand still too long you'll be left behind.

Week 3:
Find Your Key Person

Alas, you're still compiling information. You will soon realize that practically the entire process of self-promotion and self-management consists of gathering specific information on the subject. Haven't you heard the adage, "Knowledge is power"? In my opinion, there has never been a truer statement.

This is phone week, so plan to spend a lot of time on the phone. Arrange for at least one hour per day of uninterrupted phone time, away from household activities that may distract you. Now go through your list and make a brief inquiry call to each establishment to find out who is in charge of booking entertainment. That person will be your key person.

At this point it's okay to speak to nonmanagerial staff; in fact, it's best not to speak with your key person until you've gotten all the information you need. This call is only for the purpose of gathering this information. Find out the proper spelling of the key person's name, her phone extension and fax number, the best time and day to call, the mailing address, and which days of the week the establishment provides entertainment.

Avoid calling restaurants during peak hours, which are typically from 12:00 to 1:30 P.M. and 6:00 to 8:00 P.M. Early in the morning is not always a good idea either, as most restaurants are busy preparing for daily operations during that time. The slowest hours for most restaurants are usually from 2:00 to 5:00 P.M. Clubs tend to use the afternoon and early evening hours to prepare for the night's activities while no customers are present. The best time to contact most clubs is between 3:00 and 6:00 P.M.

Week 4: Record a Simple Demo Tape

Spend this week preparing a demo tape with at least four songs. Your demo doesn't need to be elaborate; an inexpensive stereo tape deck will work fine. Depending on the type of music you or your band plays, try to select songs that demonstrate your versatility. It's not necessary to record demo songs in their full length—in fact, it's best not to. A minute to a minute and a half of each song is enough. This allows the listener to get a quick overview of your band's sound. Recording a few of your best performances during rehearsal is an excellent way to produce a good demo tape. Avoid spending time on recording techniques such as "punching in" or "overdubbing"—remember, this tape will be used simply for demonstrating your band's live sound, not for selling fans.

A good habit to adopt is taking a small recorder to your gigs and recording a couple of sets. This is a great way to identify your band's strong and weak points in a performance. You may learn from your live recordings, for example, that there is too much dead time between songs, or that certain songs get the best response from the audience. These recordings can also be edited down and used for your demo.

Week 5: Prepare Your Song List, Bio, and Photo Shoot

As a newcomer, introducing yourself to a key person for the first time can have its momentary drawbacks because you have a small repertoire and no working history. Don't worry—you won't be the first or the last musician with a repertoire of only 25 songs and a three-hour gig tomorrow night. This is especially difficult for solo musicians. Some music forms, such as jazz, allow you to stretch your songs with a little imagination. Improvisation has saved me many times in the past. If you find yourself with a long gig, 25 songs will be enough to get you through at least one set, and then you'll have to repeat the set (changing the sequence of the songs, of course). After that, make sure your band rehearses new material for your next gig.

Take preliminary notes as you begin compiling personal information to be included in your bio. A bio is not much different from a job resume: you can list accomplishments, goals, and any noteworthy information that might interest a potential prospect.

As a final assignment for this week, devote some time and attention to obtaining an 8 x 10–inch, black-and-white glossy photo that best represents you or your band. Apart from searching through local phone listings, your best bet for finding a credible photographer is to ask other bands to refer one to you. An anonymous call to a local booking agent can also gain you ample information regarding local professional photographers and photo duplication outlets.

Refer to Chapter 3 for a more in-depth discussion on bios and press kits.

Life as a musician/performing artist can offer many options and alternate paths of indecision. The following is an assortment of practical outlets through which you can earn money using your music, related talents, and resources. However, it is impossible for a book to predict a band's earning potential because this depends on many variables, including the band's history and local status and the economic conditions in their city. (For a guide to determining your own earning potential, see Chapter 4, "Pricing Your Performances.")

 *Always have your press kit available when you pursue work, as you may be requested to submit one. Lack of such promotional materials can counteract your efforts, creating unnecessary holdups in securing work.*

Charities and Fund-Raisers

The American Red Cross, the American Lung Association, scholarship foundations, and public-access television networks are a diminutive sample of the many charity and nonprofit organizations that regularly host fund-raisers. Nonprofits usually have an entertainment budget starting at absolute zero, and often reserve primary funds for headliner acts. This doesn't necessarily mean that a fee can't be negotiated. As a note of encouragement, charity functions do offer a large audience with which to network. Bands are usually selected by board members or a committee assembled specifically for this purpose. These board members or committees review press packages submitted by bands or consider those with a well-known reputation. You will need to contact the organization hosting the festival or charity event to find out how press kit submissions are handled.

Bookstore and Café Gigs

Bookstore and café gigs have captured a surprisingly large share of the market, offering an atmosphere that appeals to a wide range of people. The ambience in bookstores and cafés draws an excellent audience base that you can build upon. Categorized as low-pressure gigs, they're an excellent way to break in as a newcomer. Although the primary objective of any retail outlet is to profit from the sale of goods, events like book signings, seminars, and live music performances supply added drawing power to gain the steady interest of the public.

Getting booked for the first time is not a difficult task, but getting subsequent bookings will depend on your initial performance. If you or your combo have a problem performing at low volume levels, you should avoid this type of gig altogether. Your bookstore or café performance should remain low-key—quite opposite to a gig in a bar, where your music is the focal point. Contact the person responsible for scheduling activities; bookstores often have a "community relations" person. Whenever possible, it is always best to meet in person. Make an initial inquiry with a sales clerk or other personnel; it's highly likely that the key person will be occupied with staff or other store activities and request that you stop in later, in which case, be sure to do so. In any event, leave them your card and press kit and, above all, remember to follow up with them.

Trade Shows, Conventions, and Conferences

Trade shows, conventions, and conferences present the ultimate networking environment, lasting several days with a turnout of thousands of participants and patrons from all over the country. These types of events take place in large cities with a highly concentrated focus on a particular industry. Certain trade shows and conventions are aimed specifically at the music industry and can be hotbeds for exposure, providing networking possibilities that could change the direction of your music career. You'll want to submit your press kit to trade-show or conference directors and coordinators. A good demo tape, or the finished product, is invaluable for obtaining these gigs.

If you've ever attended a trade show, such as NAMM (National Association of Music Merchants), you'll understand why technology is moving us toward a paperless environment. Scores of printed pamphlets, flyers, and brochures can quickly become a cumbersome handful as attendees pursue the nearest trash receptacle just out of your immediate eyesight. At the show, consider distributing a single-page document instead of a full-blown press package. Compile a list of possible prospects and mail them your demo when you get home to re-establish contact. To make the most of your new contacts, draw out your communication efforts as much as possible. In essence, attempt to establish a relationship or some common interest to keep communication channels open.

Symphony Gigs

For many nonunion musicians, the thought of performing with the symphony rarely materializes to any great significance. Clouded by biased views and indifference, this myopic perception of the symphony musician seems largely due to lack of information. Although it's rare, the nonunion musician can occasionally perform alongside her illustrious counterparts. In emergency situations only, when there is no qualified union member with a special skill or experience with an unusual instrument, the union may allow a nonunion musician to perform. Understandably, union members may oppose the idea of a nonunion musician receiving the same benefits as paying members. This is a popular argument that should be considered by both sides. Ultimately, if you aspire to perform with the symphony, you should consider joining the union.

Holidays and Festivals

Few countries in the world have greater diversity in cultures, music, and celebrations, all unique by-products of the American multicultural experience. The rise of "world music" record labels has escalated public awareness of, and appreciation for, other cultures. Holidays and festivals occur year-round but, of course, not every holiday is a money-making prospect for musicians. Presidents' Day and Groundhog Day hardly qualify as peak seasons, but nonetheless, there are a few holidays that seem to be designated just for music and entertainment.

While Christmas seems to be the holiday for merchants and manufacturers, New Year's Eve reciprocates as the monetary restitution for almost all working musicians. Independent musicians and bands can often negotiate for as much as triple their usual price for New Year's Eve gigs, without so much as a grimace from club and restaurant owners—this is all but impossible any other time of year. It's as if the individual writing the check is momentarily transformed into the born-again Scrooge, from the Charles Dickens tale *A Christmas Carol.*

There is a variety of holidays throughout the year that encourage live music and festive celebration. Magazines that cover any form of music often list summer concerts and annual music festivals. Since many clubs and restaurants have an increased workload preparing for festival seasons, be sure to seal your arrangements well in advance with a signed contract. Competition from other bands trying to secure seasonal gigs can be furious, and a club or restaurant owner may be tempted not to honor a verbal commitment with you in hopes of getting a premier band for that evening.

Wedding Receptions and Private Parties

Wedding receptions and private gigs, sometimes referred to as "casuals," offer a broad range of flexibility in negotiation. Unlike club dates, wedding receptions and casuals occur infrequently. Without the benefit of nightly performances to perpetuate a following, building a reputation for these types of gigs relies heavily on your band's professional presentation, word of mouth, and public accessibility. In other words, the public is not interested in a band they don't see or hear.

Wedding receptions typically require the band to wear formal attire, such as tuxedos or dark suits. Most casuals fall in the category of "black tie" affairs. For the majority of wedding receptions, I have found that the banquet manager is often very busy and suggests that the band keep an eye on the photographer for cues regarding ceremonial activities such as cutting the cake or tossing the bouquet. Pay close attention, because sometimes the band is asked to announce each activity to the wedding guests as the evening progresses. If your band is interested in these types of gigs over bars, night clubs, and restaurants, be sure to print "Weddings and Private Parties" on your business cards.

Supper Clubs, Piano Bars, and Restaurants

Supper clubs and restaurants are similar in that both focus on the dining experience. The difference is that supper clubs place an equal emphasis on liquor sales. In their dual role of restaurant and club, supper clubs encourage patrons to linger and indulge by exploiting the medium of live music.

Working the supper club/piano bar/restaurant scene has a few unique advantages over the other choices. In addition to the fact that the majority of these gigs evolve into long-term jobs, the odds of working more than one night per week are usually higher. The regular clientele at a supper club or restaurant plays a key role for you in gaining a firm foothold as a permanent fixture at the establishment.

Humans, being creatures of habit, rarely welcome change after growing accustomed to a regular routine. You are likely to step into this type of gig as a replacement for a previous regular act with a good reputation and big shoes to fill. In a case like this, your objective should be not only to please the owner but to win over the regular patrons as well. Compensate for what you lack in repertoire with your personality and talent. In contrast to the distance an elevated nightclub stage can create, the supper club places you in a more intimate position with an audience. As clientele gather around a piano bar or engage in quiet conversation and dinner just a few short feet away from you, your ability to entertain and paint a backdrop with music is of paramount importance.

Approach a supper club or restaurant by making yourself available as a sub. Typically these establishments keep a list of available subs, or stand-ins, that they call when their primary performer is booked elsewhere. It would be to your advantage to make your presence and availability known by occasionally stopping in during peak evening hours. Get acquainted with the current performer and regular clientele, but be sensitive to the fact that it's someone else's gig.

Nightclubs

Since the birth of disco, the codependence of nightclubs and live music has been undermined somewhat by DJ-oriented music forms, such as the currently popular techno and hip-hop. However, there is still great diversity in nightclubs—the selection includes jazz, swing, country and western, Top 40, oldies, hip-hop, rap, funk, rock, blues, rhythm and blues, metal, and punk, not to mention the broad range of ethnic clubs.

The nightclub circuit is not much different than most bar gigs, with the exception of a higher pay scale and less austere settings. You'll still need to submit a press kit and demo tape. Some clubs may request an audition to see how your band performs in front of an audience. Your biggest challenge might be getting the other band members to agree to these arrangements. Sending a videotape is optional but can prove to be valuable in persuading a nightclub owner to book you or your band.

 *Although gigs on weekend nights pay better at most clubs, you can opt for a weeknight to get your foot in the door.*

Happy-Hour Gigs

Happy hour usually lasts two hours, typically from 5:00 P.M. to 7:00 P.M. The musician who plays a happy-hour gig should consider himself fortunate. A happy-hour gig will usually afford you the opportunity to book a second gig later that same evening. Not all clubs promote a happy hour, but those that do are well worth looking into. I suggest checking out major hotel chains that have nightclubs or piano bars. Clubs and piano bars housed in high-rise office buildings make excellent candidates for happy-hour spots, too, because these locations have a steady flow of early-evening clientele with the business executives just getting off work. Happy-hour gigs are especially suitable for solo or duo acts. It's a good idea to work up a small duo or solo act for the times when your full band is not working steadily. If your solo or duo is good enough, you could stay busy almost as much as you'd like. Don't expect to get the same fee for a happy-hour gig as you would for a full evening, however. Look at happy hour as sort of an appetizer and not the main course.

Bars

For some reason, the general public assumes that bars are the most common environment for just about every musician. Occasionally, when I talk to people at the club where I perform on weekends, I hear the response, "We don't go to bars." It can be frustrating when people react to the name of an establishment that includes the words "wine bar" or "supper club." Bars have acquired an unfavorable reputation, associated with terms like "sleazy," "sin den," or "gutbucket," and generally don't hold a very high level of social acceptance. Bar owners hold a comparable reputation in the eyes of many working musicians. Often these establishments test the limitations of city ordinances, requiring bands to play up until the last possible moment before closing.

Sub Work

Staying busy as a sub requires versatility, even if you choose to stay in one particular musical genre. The more versatile you are, the more likely you are to be called on often. For jazz or any other music style, it's best to have a well-rounded knowledge of popular standards.

The ability to offer more than one option as a musician will greatly increase your workload. If you don't usually sing lead, consider doing background vocals, or learn to play improvised lead solos if you're accustomed to playing only rhythm parts. Visit spots where other bands and musicians are performing and make them aware of your interest in possible sub work. By all means, leave a business card.

Solo Gigs

Doing a solo gig, especially if you're good, means you can step into moneymaking situations that most bands can only imagine. The solo performer can fit within the tightest of budgets and come out making a hefty profit. You must be especially concerned with the extent of your repertoire and your ability to entertain, as all eyes will be on you for three or four hours. Once you've mastered that, your bargaining and negotiating power will be greatly enhanced.

Efficient and self-contained solo performers could be considered the workhorses of local music markets. For years the most popular solo instrument was piano. Since the advent of computers, as I'll explain shortly, that has all changed, creating seemingly endless solo possibilities for guitarists, singers, saxophonists, and a host of other instrumentalists to get into the act.

I recall a time when, for about three months, I had to play two gigs back-to-back three days a week—one at a supper club for happy hour and the other at a restaurant—with only 30 minutes between them. Luckily, they were less than a mile apart. It was challenging, but I was able to orchestrate a workable solution by having two setups, one for each location. After playing my last note at the supper club I would immediately throw my guitar in its case and head out for the next gig. My second set of gear was already set up and ready to go. What it amounted to was that I played for five straight hours, was finished by 10:00, and still had time to stop and listen to some of the other local musicians before going home for the evening. If you have the stamina, a solo routine can be a winning ticket in the local music scene.

Start Your Own "Virtual Band"

I have heard many accounts of young musicians saying, "I used to play, but my band broke up so I don't play anymore." With today's technology, that excuse is no longer valid. Putting together a solo act for small clubs, restaurants, or private parties is easier than ever. Through the use of MIDI (musical instrument digital interface) and the personal computer, the music industry has exploded with many new performers and recording artists who might otherwise never have been able to enter the music industry.

MIDI allows all MIDI-compatible devices to communicate with each other. MIDI information, in the form of sequences called Standard MIDI Files, provides the musical backdrop against which the soloist can perform. Even many major recording artists use a combination of MIDI sequences and live musicians during major concerts. On a personal computer with the proper software, MIDI files can be created and edited with ease and versatility.

MIDI has literally given musicians an almost limitless palette of instruments, allowing the user recording and live-performance potential never before imaginable. With a sequencer, laptop, or personal computer, a soloist or band can now perform fully accompanied by a three-piece combo or an entire orchestra. There are several programs on the market that are specially designed for accompaniment and are very easy to use. If you already own a personal computer with a sound card you can set yourself up with an accompaniment program very inexpensively. If you are not able to put together a band at the moment, by all means consider this as an option, or even as a sideline if you already have a band. You will be surprised at how easy it is to put together a virtual band and make extra money at the same time.

KEEP YOUR BAND WORKING

Try these simple suggestions to generate possible bookings for upcoming months. Don't let your last gig of the month sneak up on you followed by a three- or four-week gap in your calendar. Put these ideas into action at least three weeks before your last scheduled gig.

• Make follow-up calls to prospects who have expressed an interest in hiring you for an upcoming date but never confirmed it. Follow through and ask what their plans are.

• Contact former clients, clubs, and restaurants you have worked for in past months. Inform them that you are working on next month's calendar and would like to know if their entertainment arrangements have already been made.

• Show up at locations where you have performed before, not to solicit business but simply to show your face. Your unexpected presence at the club will remind the owner to consider booking you again.

Negotiating payment arrangements in the bar scene has produced some colorful and creative options. Here are some common choices you are most likely to encounter. Depending on your band's popular appeal, you may wish to adopt one or more of these methods to best suit your circumstances.

Per-Person Rates

The common phrase is, "I only pay 50 bucks per person," spoken with a certain frankness. A bar owner may sometimes choose to offer to pay per person at a rate as low as $50, with a limit, or ceiling price, of about $250 total. However, it's most likely the ceiling price won't be reached until a six- or seven-piece band shows up.

Guaranteed Base (Flat Rate)

This method differs from a per-person rate in that the bar owner offers a guaranteed base, or flat rate, that is independent of the number of band members. A bar with a large clientele may reserve these terms for bands that have a good reputation and following.

Playing for the Door or a Percentage of the Door

Playing for the door can be risky for a relatively new band that doesn't yet have a following. It puts the risk in your lap and not the club owner's. Let's say that the club agrees to pay your band 80% of the door. Two factors are at work here: (1) it's likely that the club doesn't do terrific business, at least in terms of offering a guarantee to a live band; (2) there is now a cover charge imposed, and unless the bar has a good reputation as a great weekend spot, customers can be turned off by having to pay a cover charge to hear a band they are not familiar with. It is common to negotiate a combination of a flat rate plus the door or a percentage of the door.

The bottom line is the risk of your band not getting paid enough to make it worth your while. You will find that many small bars book bands exclusively on this arrangement. If you decide to go this route, give yourself two to three weeks before the gig to post fliers and contact friends. Ask the management what type of advertising they are willing to do for your upcoming gig.

Playing for Tips

This type of arrangement should be based on your own judgment, but it could damage your reputation. If you're not concerned about getting paid, then go for it! For the purposes of supplementing your income and establishing a reputation in the local music scene, it's a bad idea. Unless you're from a wealthy family, live at home with mom and dad, or just happen to own the club or restaurant where you're playing, avoid this arrangement. Playing for tips can be a demeaning proposition and an insult to the integrity of other hard-working musicians.

Playing for Exposure

From a local perspective, playing for exposure—that is, for no money—is a necessary practice for a new band, but it is only worthwhile when it will truly increase your band's chances for more profitable performance opportunities. Be careful not to get caught up in too many gigs for the purpose of exposure. There are many clubs and individuals that would love the opportunity to book a band on the promise of exposure and make money from it. Keep in mind that someday your band will outgrow the need to generate local exposure. As you become attuned to this you will eventually realize when your band has performed enough solely for the purpose of exposure and decide to take only paying gigs.

Pay-to-Play

Although this is not a widespread practice, the pay-to-play rule should serve as a reminder of how not to make your living in music. As appalling as this arrangement sounds, it usually entails a club owner or promoter requiring a band to prepurchase tickets at a cost of, say, $3 to $5 apiece. The band then sells the tickets to friends, relatives, and strangers at a slightly higher price. Any profit over the original cost of the tickets goes to the band. This takes the risk off the club owner or promoter and places it squarely on the shoulders of the band. It's an unfair and shady proposition for the band.

There have been many heated arguments and discussions about this slap-in-the-face approach. Don't believe that the only way you or your band will ever have the chance to perform in a club is under pay-to-play terms. It's just not true! That these terms come about at all is largely due to the attitude and mindset of some club owners and promoters, but you can take comfort in the fact that it hasn't become a standard practice in the industry.

Despite their tarnished reputation, bars have played an important role in the development of bands. Fondly referred to as the "chitlin" circuit, old-school musicians proudly hail those low-paying gigs in undesirable settings as "paying one's dues."

NINE STEPS BEFORE BOOKING A PRIVATE GIG

By private gig, I mean an engagement contracted by a private individual or corporate entity, or some other function that excludes the general public. When booking private gigs, you should follow some basic steps to ensure the best possible results between you and your client. These steps are as follows:

- Get the key person's (client's) full name and the correct spelling.

- Know the type of engagement.

- Get the key person's mailing address and at least two phone numbers.

- Confirm the date and the start and finish times of the engagement.

- Know the location and address of the engagement.

- If possible, get a phone number for the engagement location and the name of a contact person there, e.g., the caterer, host, manager, etc.

- Obtain a fee deposit (at least 20% of your total fee).

- Get a signed contract.

TIPS FOR WEDDING RECEPTIONS

Wedding receptions have their own rules and formalities. Refer to these tips if your band is booked for a wedding reception.

- Be sure to make a note of the bride's and groom's names.

- Occasionally the bride and groom will request a specific song for their first dance. Make a special effort to learn it, or a similar choice.

- Throughout the reception, visually and verbally communicate with your host (key person). This will usually be the bride, the groom, or a family member.

- Often the photographer will keep the band abreast of activities during the reception, such as the first dance, cutting the cake, throwing the bouquet, etc. Pay close attention during each of these formalities. You may be asked to accompany these things with particular songs, such as the theme from *The Newlywed Game*, "What Are You Doing for the Rest of Your Life?" or "We've Only Just Begun."

- During break time, stay out of the way of guests. Occasionally the host will have a designated area for the band to go during breaks.

- Be sure to discuss meal arrangements during your initial meeting.

- If you booked the gig, make sure the host gives the check to you, not another band member.

- If the gig is booked several months in advance, call your client about one week before the wedding. The purpose of this call is to put the client at ease and confirm any last-minute details.

OTHER WAYS TO MAKE MONEY IN YOUR LOCAL MUSIC SCENE

The variety of ways to make money from your music and music-related skills is limited only by your imagination. You may already know someone who makes a living or earns extra income using one or more of the following methods.

Private Music Lessons

As long as there is music there will always be opportunities to teach it. Without a doubt, there is money to be made in teaching private music lessons. You might be surprised by the number of performing musicians who double as private teachers as a sideline. Because of today's broad range of musical styles and techniques, each year gives rise to yet another teaching method or a newly popularized instrument, making private lessons an even more prevalent trend among aspiring musicians.

Taking on students will require good organizational skills and dedication. Most teachers charge around $10 per 30-minute lesson, with one lesson per week for each student, and have a typical load of 25 to 50 students. On the low end, at 25 students, that's $250 a week, or $1,000 a month. Teaching private lessons is a very lucrative business and can generate a lot of income for a musician who doesn't want to spend a lot of time performing or booking gigs. On the other hand, teaching and performing are also an excellent combination. Not only is it financially rewarding to reap the benefits of a dual income, but for the performing musician, advertising lessons is all but unnecessary. Your public visibility as a performer becomes your own unique advertising campaign as you win the hearts of potential students young and old.

Rent Out Your Home Studio

If you own recording equipment, it's easy to earn extra money by making your recording facilities available to other musicians and songwriters. Many musicians are also talented songwriters but don't own the recording equipment to produce a demo. Offering your services on a limited basis is as easily done by posting notices on music-store bulletin boards or simply through word of mouth. With professional studio rates unaffordable for many musicians, your facilities could be workable solution for a fraction of the cost.

Rent Out Your Sound Equipment

Depending on how much equipment you have accumulated over the years, you might possess a small money-making outlet in your own garage. How about that old P.A. system or amplifier you don't use any more? Look around and see how much sound equipment you have hidden away collecting dust. There's no harm in posting fliers or simply putting the word out that you have P.A. equipment for rent. Sound-equipment rental can be very lucrative, as it literally pays for itself over and over again.

Note the makes and models of your equipment, and then contact a few music stores and ask what their fee is for a system similar to yours. Do this as if you were a potential customer, without revealing your intentions of cashing in on a part of their business. After finding out your competitors' rental rates, you can set yours slightly lower. When you are ready to do business with local bands, make sure they know that your prices are less than music-store rates.

Another benefit you can offer above your music-store competitors is after-hours services. If a P.A. system is going to crash it will most likely occur right before or during a gig. For after-hours services, you can charge extra for personally delivering and setting up a piece of sound equipment. Your ability to offer these extended services beyond competing music stores is very valuable to working bands and justifies additional compensation.

Act As an Agent for Other Bands

Do you handle all the booking for your band? How many times have you turned down a gig because your band was busy on a particular night? Booking bands other than your own can make you money and provide a valuable service for other musicians at the same time. The next time someone wants to hire your band for an evening when you're already booked, don't turn the gig down. Get the information you normally would for your own band and tell the prospect that you will provide a band for their function.

Start compiling a list of musicians and singers of all types. Make sure they are dependable and professional musicians that you can trust to hire for an engagement. Ask if they would be interested in some occasional extra work. Be sure you have enough musicians to call on that you can compose a small combo or a variety of solo acts. After you have booked an engagement, provide your client with a contract as you would for your own band. Collect a 15- to 20-percent deposit and retain that as your agent fee. Be sure to keep track of any income earned through outside bookings. Like regular band members, if you have earned more than $600 from any individual, you will need to report that income to the IRS at the end of the year. (See "Tax Concerns for the Working Musician" in Chapter 2.)

Sell Your Music at Your Gigs

Packaging and selling your music at gigs can be a hearty source of additional income. You may choose to spend a little extra money in a recording studio or to take a more cost-effective approach with just a DAT recorder and a stereo mic setup at a live performance. Either way, the end result is product, and it's for sale! As your audience grows, so does the potential to increase your income.

The benefits of having a recording are many. Though not on the grand scale of superstar recording artists, having a recording released gives the public and your potential employers the perception that you are successful. It will place you a notch above the crowd of musicians and bands in your area that have not yet achieved your status. From a simple bookstore or coffee shop to a large club gig your selling potential is demonstrated by the applause you receive from delighted and appreciative audience members.

Stay abreast of recording industry trends and techniques. Keep an eye on music-related magazines that focus on the recording musician. These publications feature articles and reviews on the latest recording techniques, trends, and products. Talk to other musicians who record. You will probably find a few tech-heads in your area who eat, sleep, and drink the recording process and would spend their last dollar on the latest and greatest gadgets for their home studios. If you run across one of these people, add them to your list of contacts and ask lots of questions. They may become instrumental in making your first recording project a success from a technical standpoint.

Be sure to bring copies of your finished product to your gigs. The benefit of selling your tapes off the stage is that you don't have to be an adept salesperson. If your audience likes you they will buy your music, right there on the spot. Make arrangements with the club owner to set up a small merchandise table in an out-of-the-way location inside the club. Have someone you trust handle this task during your band's performance, and offer her a small percentage of each sale.

MUSIC-RELATED JOBS

These are some suggestions to help you start thinking about ways you can use your musical skills professionally. Do some investigation of your own and see what other ideas you can come up with.

- Score arranger

- Music-store clerk

- Record-store clerk

- Professor of music

- Private teacher

- Church musician

- Church music director

- Jingle writer

- Studio musician

- Recording engineer

- Audio-store clerk

- Music therapist

- Booking agent

FINDING A REGULAR OLD DAY JOB

Working a regular day job is not a bad thing, although some musicians feel that it's not such a good thing, either. But as an extra source of income to help with little things like utility bills or even food, a day job can be your life preserver as you pave the road to a gratifying music career.

The musician who earnestly seeks non-music-related employment could be put in a frustrating position. No matter how popular you are as a local musician or what the degree of your musical accomplishments is, in the job market you will most likely be labeled and judged before you can fill out the first line on an application. It's a good idea to have two different resumes—one that includes your experience as a musician, which you can use for places like music stores or record stores, and another that downplays your music career for non-music-related jobs.

During an interview, you don't need to refer to your band or other musical activities unless an interviewer asks. Avoid talking too eagerly about your music career, as this could lead an interviewer to believe that your music will take a higher priority and consequently not offer you the job. Make every effort to project a professional persona. Be on time, dress neatly, and make a good first impression. Think of yourself not as a musician looking for a job but as a typical individual. Leave things at home that may identify you as a free-spirited musician, such as jewelry, chains, or ornaments. You must avoid giving a potential employer an excuse not to hire you.

WHAT DID WE LEARN?

- Consider it an achievement if you successfully convince a business to try live music for the first time.

- Devote some time and attention to obtaining an 8 x 10–inch, black-and-white glossy photo of yourself or your band.

- Always have your press kit available.

- Happy-hour gigs are especially suitable for solo or duo acts.

- Learn to anticipate the months to follow.

- Try to stay at least three months ahead in your booking schedule.

- For a relatively new band, playing for the door can be very risky.

- Playing for tips can be a demeaning proposition that insults the integrity of other hard working musicians.

- From a local perspective, playing for exposure as a relatively new band is a necessary practice, but only if it will lead to better opportunities.

- During wedding-reception gigs, keep a watchful eye on the bride and groom, the couple's parents, the photographer, and the banquet manager for cues regarding ceremonial activities throughout the reception.

- During a non-music-related job interview, avoid referring to your band or activities as a musician unless an interviewer asks.

CHAPTER 8

Bits and Pieces

T his section covers an assortment of topics that could each very well merit its own book. Although these subjects would require extended study in order to thoroughly understand them, I've include these brief overviews to accommodate the truly inquisitive musician. Here I have gone directly to the source, speaking with professionals in specific fields. Entertainment attorney Wallace Collins was extremely helpful in answering some of the common legal questions concerning bands and musicians.

THE VALUE OF A TRADEMARK

Throughout the years classic names have evolved from young, aspiring bands not much different from yours. When they started out, certainly, none of them had the slightest idea of the cultural impact and marketing potential their names would hold long after their bands ceased to exist. It's difficult to predict the outcome or success of any band or its affect on the music industry. Many highly successful bands that have recorded and toured and perhaps had a major hit record have taken a businesslike approach by incorporating and trademarking their name. This strategy leads to a whole new world of possibilities. A band that is incorporated, if represented properly, can project an image of great importance. An incorporated band is recognized as an independent, legal entity, which shields each band member from legal or tax-related repercussions that may result from unsuccessful business dealings.

An incorporated band can be more appealing to a potential investor interested in buying shares. An experienced investor may see money-making potential above and beyond record sales and song royalties that the band itself might not even recognize. If an incorporated band with a trademarked name becomes successful—even if the band breaks up—investors still have the potential to make money through licensing the name to manufacturers or other corporate entities that have a commercial interest in the trademarked name.

With the understanding that incorporating and trademarking a name generates a huge number of additional responsibilities, it is clearly best to seek the aid of an attorney that specializes in corporations and trademarks. It's not worth the expense and effort to trademark or incorporate unless your band has gained some level of success. Only after you have released a recording (whether independently or under a record label that aggressively promotes your CD), as well as achieved good airplay and significant record sales, should you consider this step.

HOW TO COPYRIGHT YOUR MUSIC

For a new songwriter, the excitement of hearing one's creation come to life can be overwhelming, sometimes causing one to overlook a very important element of songwriting: copyrights! Copyrighting your songs today will save you a lot of trouble and heartache tomorrow. The copyright procedure is not difficult, yet it is the most important step in protecting your songs.

Register your songs with the Library of Congress's U.S. Copyright Office using the PA (Performing Arts) form. The fee for a copyright as of this printing is $20 per song. This could become costly, depending on the number of songs you want to copyright, but you can get around this. Songs can be copyrighted individually or collectively using only one form. For example, you can group several songs that are on one cassette or CD and title them "The Collective Works of [your name]." This method will save you money, but you must be sure to keep track of which songs you include in your submission. Write to: U.S. Copyright Office; Library of Congress; 101 Independence Avenue, S.E.; Washington, D.C. 20559-6000. Or call the copyright forms and information 24-hour hot line: (202) 707-3000. You can also download and print out copyright forms as needed from http://lcweb.loc.gov/copyright.

Your best legal defense is thorough documentation of all your important business dealings. Create a file for important activities you are engaged in, and keep in it copies of business-related letters and other correspondence that you have written or received. When you submit demo tapes to record companies, retain an exact copy of the submitted materials in your file, along with all related receipts for postage, copy services, etc. In essence, these documents are all evidence that certain activities did in fact take place regarding particular business dealings, and they will protect you in the event of copyright infringement.

A great concern to songwriters and recording musicians is finding an entertainment lawyer. For songwriters, another issue is the question of works made for hire: *Who owns the songs?* The following two articles were written by New York entertainment lawyer Wallace Collins. Mr. Collins was very helpful in answering the commonly asked legal questions covered in this chapter (see page *118*) and was kind enough to write the forward to this book and allow me to reprint the following. *Thanks, Wallace.*

AN ENTERTAINMENT LAWYER'S VIEW ON COPYRIGHTS AND WORKS MADE FOR HIRE

The Implication of Work Made for Hire

Most record contracts require that recording artist render their services to their record labels pursuant to a "work made for hire" provision. Under the work-made-for-hire doctrine of the U.S. copyright law, the record label retains ownership of an artist's master recordings and thus ensures maximum profits for itself.

However, the legal ramifications of these work-made-for-hire arrangements could be disastrous for the record industry. Most labels could face substantial liability under the Federal Fair Labor Standards Act and under New York and California state labor laws, since the artists who create works made for hire could be deemed employees for the purposes of workers' compensation benefits, minimum-wage guarantees, and unemployment and disability insurance. There may also be grounds for an artist employee to revoke existing contracts, a move that could be especially devastating to a record label that has an option for future works from an artist.

Under the U.S. copyright law, as amended by the Sound Recording Act of 1971, a copyright is granted in a sound recording separate and apart from the copyright granted in the underlying song. Copyright ownership is usually vested in the person who actually creates a given work in the moment that it is "fixed in a tangible medium," which, in the case of a recording artist, would be when the master is recorded. If the work is created as a work made for hire, then the company who hires or employs the artist is deemed to be the author of the work and owns all rights of copyright in the work.

Record contracts are structured as multi-album-recording commitments, whereby the label agrees to finance one or more albums and has the option to demand several more from the artist at the label's sole discretion. The record label "advances" a sum of money to the artist for the production of the album, which the artist records and than delivers to the record label on a work-made-for-hire basis. Assuming that the record company releases the album and that there are sales, the record company agrees to pay the artist a "royalty" from the sales of the album based on an extremely complicated calculation involving a myriad of variables. However, before the record label actually pays any royalties to the artist, it is entitled to "recoup" the entire advance solely from the artist's royalties.

Under this scenario, the artist ultimately pays for the cost of producing an album, but the record company owns the album in its entirety, and the artist receives little or no real compensation, since the bulk of the advance is used to pay for recording costs. Since the record company also has the right to cross-collateralize outstanding advances from any one album against royalties otherwise payable from any other album, an artist could conceivably sell thousands of albums and still be in an unrecouped position with its record label. All the while, however, the record company is being paid for the albums and takes its profit off the top.

Record labels justify this system largely on the basis that it protects them from the high number of failures that occur. To be fair, it is a high-stakes business; record labels do frequently end up with albums that do not sell and do not make a profit, and the label often loses its entire investment. However, the size and profitability of the major record labels clearly indicates that the system works much better for them than it does for the typical artist. That is where federal and state labor laws come into play.

Record labels and artists alike should take very seriously the possibility that their relationship is a matter of employment rather than independent contracting. Most record contracts contain numerous provisions that state that the label has the right to control the nature and quality of the artist's work and output, to control recording sessions, and to accept or reject delivered product if it is not "commercially satisfactory." The label almost always has the contractual right to exercise discretion over the artist's repertoire and the content of the recordings and can require the artist to stop recording or to rerecord any track to suit the label's standards. Furthermore, almost all significant recording contracts are "exclusive" such that the label controls the sole right to the artist's output during the term of the agreement.

All of these factors weigh in favor of a finding by the courts that the artist is the record company's employee under the Federal Fair Labor Standards Act and state labor laws, specifically those of California and New York, where most record labels are headquartered.

In the event that the artist is deemed to be the record label's employee, the artist has a variety of available rights and remedies. The artist has a right to claim workers' compensation benefits for job-related injuries and, if those injuries are severe enough, the artist may qualify for disability coverage.

Likewise, an artist whose option is not picked up by the label can claim that he was fired and may well be entitled to claim unemployment-insurance benefits.

In addition, the artist has a right to claim minimum-wage guarantees during the term of employment. A minimum-wage salary must be paid in a timely fashion, must be guaranteed, and cannot be based on the vagaries of sales figures and royalties. Failure to abide by these standards opens the record labels to claims for actual and statutory damages under the Federal Fair Labor Standards Act and other applicable labor laws.

Most significantly, a record label's failure to provide the appropriate employment benefits and wage payments may constitute grounds for rescission of the contracts on the basis that they violate public policy and are void ab initio, or are void for lack of consideration. In addition to demanding the return of the master recordings, the artist may also be able to collect consequential damages arising from the rescission of the contracts.

Such a scenario could mean an enormous windfall for recording artists and financial disaster for the record industry. Record companies would do well to carefully review the unwieldy language in the myriad provisions of their artist contracts and streamline them so as to avoid this artist-employee scenario. (Originally printed in *Billboard* magazine. Reprinted with permission from Wallace Collins.)

AN ENTERTAINMENT LAWYER'S VIEW ON ENTERTAINMENT LAWYERS

**Entertainment Lawyers:
Who? What? When?
Where? and How Much?**

As an artist in the recording industry, you do not need to know everything about the business in order to succeed, but you should hire people that do, and you should try to learn and understand what is going on around you as you go. When I was a teenage recording artist back in the late '70s, I can remember being intimidated by the "suits." Now that I'm on the other side of the desk, I have a broader perspective. I am here to tell you that those "suits" can help you; provided, however, that like any other aspect of your life, you use your instincts in making your selection.

A good place for you to start building your "team" of representatives is with a competent lawyer who specializes in entertainment law. Eventually, your team will probably include a personal manager, a booking agent, and a business manager. Your lawyer can assist you in assembling your team. He may then function as your linchpin in coordinating the activities of your team and ensuring that these people are acting in your best interest.

An entertainment lawyer will navigate you safely through the minefield that is the music business. Recording and publishing agreements can be extremely complicated, and proper negotiating and drafting requires superior legal skills as well as a knowledge of music business practice. In addition to structuring and documenting a deal to maximize the benefits to you, some lawyers also actively solicit deals for their clients by "shopping" demo tapes.

When looking for a lawyer, you should not be afraid to see a few before retaining one. Some lawyers are with large firms but many are solo practitioners. The size of the firm is not an indication of a particular lawyer's competence. Lawyers have various personalities and legal skills and you should seek out a situation where the "vibe" is right. Although your first contact may be on the telephone, most likely you will have an initial interview for which there is usually a charge. Remember, your lawyer's time is money, so be prepared and be on time for your appointment.

It helps if your lawyer likes your music but it is more important that you feel he is trustworthy and competent. The lawyer/client relationship is known as a "fiduciary" relationship, which means that a lawyer must always act in your best interest and not his own or that of anyone else. Your lawyer is also under a duty to keep your conversations with him confidential. It is often in your best interest that it stays that way.

Keep in mind that a lawyer with other big-name clients is not necessarily the best lawyer for you; if it comes down to taking your calls or those of a superstar, which do you think will get preference?

You are probably wondering how much a lawyer costs. Well, remember that the only thing a lawyer has to sell is his time. A lawyer, much like a doctor, is selling services, so if you go to him for advice, you should expect to pay. With the odds of success in this business being what they are, very few lawyers will agree to work for you and wait for payment until you are successful and can pay your bills.

An entertainment lawyer usually charges an hourly fee for a percentage of the money value of your deal. Hourly rates run from $125 to $250 and up. Percentages are based on the "reasonable value of services rendered" and generally run around five percent of the deal. A few lawyers may charge a set fee, such as $1,000 or $1,500, to review and negotiate certain documents. Check around to see if the fee arrangement proposed is competitive.

Most lawyers will require that you pay a retainer. In addition to the hourly fee or percentage, you are usually required to reimburse your lawyer for his out-of-pocket costs, including long-distance telephone calls, photocopies, postage, faxes, etc.

You should realize that in retaining a lawyer, you are making a contract even if your agreement is not written. In return for a fee, the lawyer promises to render legal services on your behalf. However, some lawyers may want a fee arrangement in writing (specifically in the demo-shopping situation). A cautious lawyer will advise you that you have the right to seek the advice of another lawyer as to the propriety of the fee arrangement.

Since an entertainment lawyer is often in a position to access record companies, you may want to have your lawyer "shop" your demos. Such arrangements can be time-consuming for the lawyer. There are other problems with such arrangements, not the least of which are potential conflict-of-interest problems. It is beyond the scope of this article to deal with all of the intricacies of tape shopping arrangements. Basically, such an agreement will have an exclusive term of 6 to 12 months, require a retainer of between $1,000 and $5,000 plus expenses, and grant the layer a percentage of the deal ranging from five to ten percent. Keep in mind that there is no guarantee of success. No matter how enthusiastically your lawyer hustles on your behalf, or how much supposed "clout" your lawyer has, it is still up to the discretion of the record label whether to sign you.

As a general rule, you need a lawyer if you are asked to sign anything other than an autograph. Too many aspiring artists want to get a record deal so badly that they will sign almost anything that promises them a chance to do it. Even successful careers have a relatively short life span. Therefore, it is important for you to get maximum returns in the good years and not sign away rights to valuable income, like publishing.

Never sign anything without having a lawyer review it first. Do not rely on anyone else to tell you what your contract says. Your lawyer will translate the deal for you and explain to you exactly what you are getting into. Do not let anyone rush you or pressure you into signing any agreement. There is really no such thing as a standard form contract. Any such contract was drafted by that party's attorney to protect that party's interest; your lawyer can help negotiate more favorable terms for you. Everyone needs someone to look out for his or her interests. That is why you need a lawyer. (Originally printed in *Music Business Monthly Report*. Reprinted with permission from Wallace Collins.)

Q. What is the difference between a contract and a letter of agreement? Which one carries the most weight in court?

A. *There is no legal difference between a contract and a letter of agreement; these are merely different names for written documents. Legally, a contract, whether written or oral, is an "offer" by one party that is "accepted" by another party for "consideration" (e,g., an agreement to pay for something).*

Q. What if a copyright case goes to court? How should one prepare?

A. *Other than filing a copyright registration form, there is really no way to prepare. That is for your trial lawyer to do.*

Q. If a band has recorded for a record label and a member decides to go her own way, is she still obligated to the band or the record label?

A. *There is not much the band can do to prevent a particular member from leaving. As for the record contact, every record contract I ever negotiated (even after it was negotiated) said that each member was bound to the label individually and collectively—so a member could leave the band but not the label.*

Q. Can a band get out of a record contract if the label is not actively promoting the band or have not shown any interest for a great length of time?

A. *That is strictly a matter of what the language negotiated in the contract says. In most cases, the label has only minimal requirements (e.g., to record a record and, maybe, a commitment to release each record or else release the band from the contract)—but again, it depends on what was negotiated.*

Q. Is there some type of agreement that a band could sign that would clarify terms in the event of a split-up? If so, what is it called?

A. *In most cases, a successful band will have a written "partnership agreement" that sets forth the obligations of the band members. Otherwise, they are simply "partners" under the law of most states.*

Q. What's the best method of finding a legitimate entertainment lawyer? Is there a resource pool available, exclusively for entertainment lawyers?

A. *The best method for finding an entertainment lawyer is to get a recommendation, either from a friend or from a Bar Association referral service (such services exist in New York City and Los Angeles, for example), or by reading an article by a lawyer whose philosophy you relate to.*

Check **IT** Out! ▶ *The common element in just about all of these answers is that agreements are supported by documentation. A contract, letter of agreement, and partnership agreement are all documents that serve as the basic foundation that legally supports the terms stated therein.*

OBTAINING A BAR CODE

Your recording project, when finished, will ultimately end up in a record store and other retail outlets. To aid manufacturers and retailers in more efficient product stocking and inventory tracking, bar coding has become a standard method of product identification throughout the manufacturing and retail industries. You will need to apply for a bar code (UPC, or Universal Product Code) if you intend to commercially distribute your own finished tape or CD. As a marketing tool, some pressing plants will include a bar code as part of their sales package. To save you some steps, when you're shopping for an affordable plant to press your CDs, ask if they offer a bar code. You can go directly to the source by contacting the Uniform Code Council at (800) 543-8137, or write to: Uniform Code Council, Inc.; 8163 Old Yankee Road, Suite J; Dayton, Ohio 45458.

ABOUT PERFORMING RIGHTS ORGANIZATIONS

In order for you to get paid as a songwriter, you must first become a member of a performing rights organization. A performing rights organization keeps track of each time your music is played on radio, TV, satellite networks, etc. Joining one of these organizations is your responsibility—don't leave it up to someone else. BMI, ASCAP, and SESAC are well-established entities who will gladly send you information on how to become a member. You can only join one as a writer, and it's important to copyright your music before you take this step. BMI; 320 W. 57th Street; New York, NY 10019-3790. ASCAP; 1 Lincoln Plaza; New York, NY 10027. SESAC; 55 Music Square East; Nashville, TN 37203.

The purpose of an endorsement is to help heighten an individual's or organization's credentials and/or public appeal. Nothing can replace creditability, and if you lose it, it's very difficult to regain. The more credentials you gain, the more weight you can throw around as you evolve into one of the local heavyweights.

If your band has made any accomplishments, like opening for a well-known recording act at a major concert event, be sure to include this in your bio or other marketing materials. If you can't obtain a written endorsement or blurb, put the event in story form (using factual information, of course). Somewhere in your bio you can refer to a brief statement from or conversation you had with a big-name recording artist. It doesn't have to be anything profound. The objective is only to show that you have crossed paths with that person at some point in your music career.

The public will often perceive your brief encounter as a major accomplishment, giving your band an upscale image that could lead to higher-paying gigs and better status among your peers. Such an account may seem trivial or petty and barely worth mentioning, but it could make a difference in getting booked for other major concert events and how the local public views you from now on.

For the ambitious musician, few events can parallel a rare opportunity to stand face-to-face with a big recording star and ask her for a letter of endorsement. Although the answer will not always be yes, those who agree will make the effort worthwhile.

You will find that a great number of popular recording artists and entertainers will be understanding and willing to help you with your music career. Remember to occasionally stay in touch with them. These could turn out to be your most important contact in the music industry. After you've successfully obtained a personal endorsement you can make contact again when your band is recording and ask if they would write liner notes for your CD. If they have already written you a personal endorsement, the answer will usually be yes.

HOW MANUFACTURER ENDORSEMENTS WORK

As a new and virtually unknown musician, it's hard to obtain an endorsement of any sort. Usually when a recording band or artist gains popularity in the industry, instrument manufacturers will provide a band or an appropriate member with their products in exchange for an endorsement. Typically a band of this caliber is on the road much of the time which benefits manufacturers by exposing their instruments to the public and hopefully generating mass appeal to other musicians like yourself.

Manufacturers' endorsement programs fall into three categories: *exclusive endorsement, full endorsement, and participating-artist endorsement.* All endorsements are negotiable; some involve money and some don't. A manufacturer's greatest concern when signing a new endorser is his ability to influence product sales.

Rare in the industry, exclusive endorsements are reserved for those who have achieved superstar status. This type of endorsement usually involves a large sum of money up-front and subsequent royalties to the endorsing artist. In return, the artist grants exclusive use of her name and likeness in association with the manufacturer's product. Usually the manufacturer will produce an exclusive product that carries the endorser's name.

A full endorsement may also involve up-front payments to the artist. Money and negotiated terms vary, depending on how much influence an endorser has. A full endorsement usually involves equipment provided to the artist in exchange for his endorsement of the manufacturer's product. The manufacturer may go as far as placing the endorser's signature on a preexisting product in its line, with a few customized modifications for the new endorser.

The participating-artist endorsement can be viewed as an entry-level endorsement. Here, a manufacturer may sign a sideman musician for a larger, better-known act as a participating artist endorser. This allows the artist to buy products directly from the manufacturer at dealer cost. This type of endorsement sometimes includes paid clinics at retail outlets or guest appearances at music trade shows for brief performances and autograph signings.

Instrument manufacturers receive press kits almost daily from musicians hoping to gain an endorsement relationship. Some musicians want nothing more than discounted or free equipment. The more serious-minded musician perceives it as a career enhancement tool to create clout and influence. From a manufacturer's perspective, signing a new endorser depends on the artist's ability to influence the market and move product.

Try to put yourself in the manufacturer's position. Do you have what it takes to become an endorser? Are you signed with a record label? Do you have music currently playing on the radio and selling in record stores? Are you touring with a major artist or your own band? These are just a few things that a manufacturer will look for before signing a new endorser. Make sure your press kit brings out all of your most important accomplishments.

Sometimes your best chance of having a manufacturer consider you as an endorser is to meet face-to-face with their "artist relations" representatives. If you can afford to, try to attend one of the music industry's trade shows that take place annually. One of the largest of these trade shows is NAMM (National Association of Music Merchants). Here, you'll find major musical instrument manufacturers, software manufacturers, book publishers, and music dealers from around the world, all under one roof. The NAMM show is an excellent opportunity to meet with just about anyone in the industry. Contact NAMM show representatives for show schedules and how to attend.

OBTAINING A LICENSE TO RECORD A PREVIOUSLY RELEASED SONG

If you or your band ever has the desire to record someone else's music, the Harry Fox Agency is the first place to start in order to obtain permission and execute the necessary formalities. The Harry Fox Agency, representing more than 13,000 American music publishers, was established to provide an information source and monitoring service for licensing musical copyrights. This agency licenses a large percentage of music usage in the United States on records, tapes, and CDs and also licenses music on a worldwide basis for use in films, commercials, television programs, and all other forms of audio-visual media. If you have plans to record a previously recorded song, you need to acquire a mechanical license through the Harry Fox Agency or the original publisher. There is a fee and some brief paperwork involved.

Mechanical and Synchronization Licensing Defined:

Mechanical: The licensing of copyrighted musical compositions for use on commercial records, tapes, CDs, and computer chips to be distributed to the public for private use. This is what you will need to obtain when you want to include a previously released song on your CD.

Synchronization: The worldwide licensing of copyrighted musical compositions for use in audio-visual works, including motion pictures, broadcast and cable television programs, DVD videos, and home video games.

YOUR MUSIC AND THE INTERNET

As with every industry, growing pains play an essential role in the evolutionary process. Since the first music file was uploaded to the Internet, the record industry and the Internet have battled each other.

This rivalry has been greatly amplified as volumes of articles and editorial reports sing praises to MP3, the newest file format that converts and compresses once cumbersome Wave files down to a manageable byte size, perfect for Internet commerce. This new file format has opened the door for many unsigned bands and songwriters to profit from the sale of their music on the Web. Already, scores of new enterprises have been spawned and are ready to do business with the next generation of recording artists, offering as much as 50% of profits. Type in www.mp3.com the next time you're online.

Many of you would like to know about the American Federation of Musicians, or AFM (known in some places as the Musicians Union), and the pros and cons of becoming a member. In my personal investigation, I was pleased to discover that the AFM has a rich and intriguing history worth looking into. The AFM offers an extensive benefit package including health and life insurance, loan programs, legal services, and even a pension fund. Many world-famous entertainers are members of the AFM. Its one 100-plus-year history is proof that musicians can obtain the support they truly need. The AFM is an important entity in the music industry that should be explored by all musicians.

The union is financed by yearly membership dues and by work dues on jobs that are protected by the union. The amount of dues varies from local to local and are democratically voted on by members. The amount of dues paid to the Federation to support international offices and contracts are set by the vote of elected local representatives, who meet biennially at the AFM Convention.

HISTORIC FACTS ABOUT THE AFM

The following are various excerpts from "The AFM: The First Century," reprinted with permission from the International Musician, *the official journal of the American Federation of Musicians of the United States and Canada.*

Before there was an AFM, there was the National League of Musicians (NLM). Founded in 1886, it was the heir to the Mutual Aid Societies of the mid-1880s, which sought to counteract some of the harsher realities of working as a musician by providing loans, financial assistance during illness or extended unemployment, and death benefits.

From these roots rose the New York City–based Musical Mutual Protective Union, which, beginning in 1878, took the first step toward unionizing musicians by acting to fix uniform scales for different types of musical employment. By March 1886, delegates from 15 different prospective Unions across the United States came together to form the National League of Musicians (NLM).

The NLM grew quickly, but from the beginning it was unable to balance the contradictions inherent in a "musicians' union." It allowed the Locals to retain complete autonomy, which made curtailing competition between members from different cities impossible. And it excluded from membership musicians who didn't conform to its "artistic" standards, creating a gulf that allowed pervasive undercutting of NLM standards. It was this insistence on remaining an "organization of artists" that was the NLM's eventual undoing. The NLM dissolved at its 1904 convention, disbursing its remaining funds to its Locals.

Beginning in 1887, the American Federation of Labor (AFL) and the Knights of Labor both invited the NLM to affiliate with the trade union movement. The offers were always rejected. So both the AFL and the Knights organized their own Locals, taking in musicians who didn't meet the NLM standards. The ensuing competition among unions drove down wages for all musicians.

The NLM protested these parallel organizing efforts, but was rebuffed. To resolve this destructive situation, NLM delegates who favored trade union affiliation requested and received a charter from AFL President Samuel Gompers. In 1896, the AFM was born from the principle that all musicians who receive pay need a labor union to secure fair wages and working conditions.

In 1902 the AFM chartered its first "colored" Local, in Chicago, in keeping with laws stipulating "separate but equal" facilities of all types for African Americans. By the mid-1940s there were 50 "black" Locals in the AFM, most found in the South. These Locals were entitled to voice and vote at all AFM Conventions and had the same level of autonomy as their white neighbors. And all pursued the same union goals for the musicians they represented.

But by the early 1950s many black and white Locals were voluntarily negotiating integration agreements. As the Civil Rights movement worked toward universal integration, the AFM adopted a policy at its 1964 Convention to mandate mergers in cities where black and white Locals remained.

The negotiations were not always easy, given the concerns of black members that they would lose their representation within the union. AFM president Herman Kenyan appointed retired President James C. Petrillo and Presidential Assistant E.V. Lewis to a Civil Rights Department to oversee the mergers. By 1971, all the remaining black and white Locals were merged or rechartered. In 1977, the Convention adopted a bylaw providing for black Convention delegates from all the Locals where mergers were mandated, to assist continued representation of African Americans.

In 1927, with the release of the first "talkie," *The Jazz Singer,* the AFM had its first encounter with technological unemployment. Within three years, 22,000 theater jobs for musicians who accompanied silent movies were lost, while fewer than 200 jobs for musicians performing on soundtracks were created by the new technology over the same period. The AFM engaged in an extensive public-relations campaign to sway the public against "canned music," but the public was unconvinced and that form of employment was never recovered.

[The Recording Industries Music Performance Trust Funds was] one of the most innovative ideas in labor management relations. AFM President James C. Petrillo's plan was to secure royalties from record sales to finance a fund that employs musicians for free, live public performances and the recording ban was the weapon that eventually led to the creation of the Recording Industries Music Performance Trust Funds (Recording Industries MPTF). Since it first disbursed money in 1947, the Recording Industries MPTF has paid musicians over $500,000,000 in scale wages from negotiated fees that represent only a minuscule portion of the cost of a single record.

It was one of the oldest of musicians' dreams, dating back to the days of the Mutual Aid Societies: the dream of having a secure retirement provided for by a pension from their earnings as musicians. The realization of the dream began in January 1959, as part of the AFM's collective bargaining agreement with the recording industry. Although it was initially only provided to musicians who worked for recording companies, it was AFM President Herman Kenin's goal from the inception of the American Federation of Musicians-Employers Pension Welfare Fund...was that eventually all types of musical employment would be covered by the pension funds. Today, the potential exists for musicians to receive pension contributions for work done in every area of the business from casuals to recordings, tours to symphonies. Both the U.S. and Canadian pension funds are recognized as among the soundest in any industry and all pension contributions made to the funds are made solely by employers.

One of the greatest blows to the union's ability to represent musicians in the live single-engagement and club-date segment of the music business came in the late 1970s and early 1980s when the National Labor Relation Board and the federal courts allowed hotels, lounges, and similar venues to renounce their role as the employer of the musicians working in their establishments. Instead, the NLRB and the courts identified the leader as the employer, even when the venue set all the conditions of the employment.

These rulings destroyed the union's ability to participate in the collective bargaining process with the employers who control the single-engagement and club-date business. The AFM lost a fundamental trade union right. As a result, since 1982, the AFM has been lobbying for passage of the Live Performing Artist Labor Relations Act...to win back collective bargaining rights for short-term employment in clubs, lounges, and similar venues.

In the 1950s, with the onset of the dominance of the mass media, the union saw a serious threat to all but the most commercially viable styles of music. Jazz, folk, and especially symphonic music were vulnerable because they were most often heard in live performances produced by nonprofit arts organizations, which could not compete with the electronic media. To prevent these styles of music from becoming extinct, the AFM launched an intensive lobbying and public relations effort in 1955 aimed at preserving America's cultural heritage.

For many years, symphony, folk, and jazz musicians subsidized their own industries by working for extremely low wages while holding other jobs to make a living. Now the AFM began asking Congress and the general public to do their part in subsidizing the nonprofit arts industry through government-sponsored grants.

After a decade-long struggle led by the AFM, the National Endowment for the Arts (NEA) was created to fulfill the country's responsibility to preserve its culture. Much of the growth in the number of professional symphony orchestras and other nonprofit music programs that now bring the arts to every community in the United States is a result of the creation of the NEA.

As Baby Boomers embraced the youth culture of the 1960s, young musicians became more vulnerable to exploitation by employers. They often began their professional careers at an earlier age and with less knowledge or experience in the union than previous generations. And they were also more likely to be casualties of the union's own generation gap—ridiculed because of the music they played and distrustful of the over-30 generation that was the union.

But they still needed a union and the union needed them. In an effort to "reach and teach" young musicians about the importance of collective strength, the AFM established the Young Sounds program in 1968. Young Sounds was designed to enable young musicians to join the union at a reduced dues rate in order to receive special instructions in music and unionism, while performing for youth-oriented engagements. Despite its good intentions, today only two Locals sponsor Young Sounds programs.

It was one of the union's most publicly scorned disputes. In 1942, under the terms of the AFM's agreement with NBC radio, Petrillo ordered the network to cancel a series of concerts by students at the National Music Camp at Interlochen, Michigan, which had recently been affiliated with the University of Michigan.

The union maintained that the student concerts (which had been broadcast by NBC since 1931) were commercial in nature and therefore directly competitive with the employment of professional musicians. Therefore they were in violation of the union's closed-shop agreement with NBC. NBC complied with the "order" to stop the Interlochen broadcast, painting Petrillo as a villain in an attempt to weaken the union and its leader. Public outrage ran high against this attack on children.

The Interlochen incident had three ultimate results. It led to a Congressional investigation of the AFM—the first union to come under such scrutiny. It prompted Congress to adopt the Lea Act in 1946. And in 1947 it led to the adoption of the Music Code of Ethics between the union and the Music Educators' National Conference, which defines the rights of professional and student musicians.

It was the AFM's "noble experiment." In 1959 the AFM launched the Congress of Strings (COS)—a union-sponsored training program for young violin, viola, cello, and double bass players, to counteract the shortage of musicians qualified to perform in the symphony orchestras of the United States and Canada. During its 30-year history, some of the greatest artist in the orchestral world, including composers Roy Harris and Morton Gould, conductors Eugene Ormandy, Erich Leinsdorf, and Max Rudolf, musicians and teachers Pablo Casals, Dorothy Delay, and Gary Karr shared their talents with the students who attended the COS summer camps to advance the effort.

Before it was deemed to have fulfilled its mission and was dissolved in 1990, the Congress of Strings provided more than 3,000 students with the training that would give them the grounding they needed in performance technique and trade unionism to begin professional careers. Today there are COS alumni in virtually every symphony orchestra in the U.S. and Canada.

BECOMING AN AFM MEMBER

The AFM offers an impressive list of benefits for its members. Affiliation with the AFM can be a great asset to the serious career musician. For more information about the American Federation of Musicians and the benefits offered, contact: The American Federation of Musicians of the United States and Canada; 1501 Broadway, Suite 600; New York, NY 10036-5503. The following information is made available thanks to the assistance and efforts of the American Federation of Musicians.

Some of the Benefits of Membership

- Established minimum wages and working conditions on a local-by-local basis

- Locally and internationally negotiated contracts in many fields, including studio recording, TV, motion pictures, commercials, concerts, stage shows, symphony, opera, and ballet (pension is also available under these contracts)

- Local jobs sponsored or cosponsored by the Recording Industries Music Performance Trust Funds (RIMPTF)—a resource negotiated by the AFM and supported by contributions from recording companies

- *International Musician,* a monthly musician's trade publication that includes "help wanted" and audition notices

- Local job-referral programs

- Wage protection if a club or other employer fails to honor your AFM-approved contract

- Emergency assistance for traveling musicians

- AFL-CIO Union Privilege Program, providing special loan mortgage, credit card, and legal services

- Special rates for instrument insurance

- Special rates for life, accident, and liability insurance

- Complete list of AFM-franchised booking agents available for members' use

- AFM-organized education and legislative programs that work to protect musician's professional rights

If you have access to the Internet, take a moment to visit the AFM Web site at www.afm.org.

WHAT DID WE LEARN?

- Many highly successful bands have taken a businesslike approach by incorporating and trademarking their name.

- Songs can be copyrighted individually or collectively using one form.

- Bar coding has become a standard method of product identification throughout the manufacturing and retail industries.

- Your best legal defense is to document all important business dealings.

- In order to get paid as a songwriter, you must become a member of a performing-rights organization.

- A manufacturer's greatest concern when signing a new endorser is his or her ability to influence product sales.

- AFM stands for American Federation of Musicians.

Interviews with Real Working Musicians

I t's been a great pleasure to both know and work with most of the individuals whose personal interviews are presented here. Rarely does one obtain an intimate glimpse inside the lives of real working musicians. As you read, you will discover how true career musicians think as they explain, in their own words, their personal advice to you. I owe a special thanks to everyone for their eager participation and willingness to share their insight and experiences.

TIRK WILDER

Singer-Songwriter

What do you do, and how long have you been making your living in music?

I play every type of music I can safely cover, which includes country (of course!—I live in Oklahoma), rock (a very broad category), some blues, some pop, and a little light jazz. Music has been my main source of gainful employment since 1973, locally, and for another ten years before that in other cities.

The music I am most at home with could probably be classified as "folk." If I had my druthers, it would be me, my voice, and my guitar, doing nothing but my own stuff. It's kind of James Taylor-y, Cat Stevens-y, Gordon Lightfoot-y, or Leonard Cohen-y.

What made you decide to make your living in music?
I discovered that women are attracted to musicians.

Is there a spouse or family member involved with you in your music career? If so, who, and what does he or she do?
There is a spouse, but her only real involvement is in giving me encouragement.

What has been the highlight of your music career up to this point?
There are so many, but I guess I'd have to say it was appearing on national TV with Chuck Norris when he did my song that was about to become the theme song for his TV show *Walker, Texas Ranger.*

What has been the lowest point of your music career up to this point?
I don't know. I guess I'd have to say the times when I got unexpectedly released from a gig someplace, especially when I was barely hanging on by my financial fingernails. This happens to all of us, but the iron still burns even when other steers have a brand, too.

Have you had any particular opportunities as a direct result of your music career? If so, what?
My songwriting career has finally gotten its start. There are publishers in Nashville who will listen to the stuff I send them now. The problem is getting the tapes to sound right. Perfectionism is sometimes its own worst enemy.

If you could begin your music career all over again, what would you do differently?
Probably be more assertive and less compromising. And definitely less intimidated by record-company types. I would also work hard on getting more exposure, both for myself as an act and for my material.

What advice would you like to share with aspiring musicians?
- Don't just sit around playing your ax, waiting for some bigwig to "discover" you.
- Learn the *business* of music, and practice its edicts as much as you practice your scales.
- Learn that how well you get along with the other members of your band on a personal level is almost, if not equally, as important as how well any of you play your instruments.
- March to the beat of the drum *you* hear, no matter what anyone else tells you the cadence should be.

I should add that, at the moment, I am not actively playing anywhere for a living. I had laser surgery on my throat in 1994 and can't be around much second-hand cigarette smoke. I have another successful business that I am going to allow to provide me with a retirement, and I am getting after it. I *am* writing a lot of material and hope to get some songs covered within the next year or two. But you never know. In this business, nothing is ever set in stone....

Tirk Wilder played his first professional gig in 1963 as part of Beatles knock-off band. As part of the XLs, he played warm-up for Jerry Lee Lewis in 1965. He went on the road with a band called Stereos in 1965 and played at least a week in almost every Western state. He formed a band called the Shakers in 1966. All four members of the Shakers were capable of lead and harmony vocals. They were doing Beach Boys stuff with four guys ("Sloop John B," etc.). The Shakers' name changed to The Proof of the Puddin' and they released two singles for RCA Victor in 1967–68.

Wilder became a solo act in New Orleans circa 1971. He played on Bourbon Street in a club then called the Ivanhoe (601 Bourbon St.) from 7:00 to 10:00 P.M., after which the bands came on and played till 6:00 A.M. He played at the Wrong Place, a folk bar on the fringe of the French Quarter that, at its height, had people packed wall-to-wall every night of the week. This was a big learning experience. In the summer of 1996, the man who owned the Wrong Place had a 25-year reunion of the people who had played there and a lot of the people who had hung out there. It was held at his farm in Arkansas, and it came off like a mini-Woodstock.

In 1974, Wilder moved to Oklahoma City. He appeared on Channel 4's *Danny's Day* talk show seven times. He played in local clubs too numerous to enumerate, but these include the Nomad II, the Raintree Lounge, Sugar's Mai Kai, the Red Lady Lounge, and the Schnappskellar. He has also played hundreds of private parties, wedding receptions, and grand openings and played at the Elks' Golf & Country Club in Duncan, Oklahoma.

Wilder played keyboard for the Easy Money Band in 1988. The lead singer of that band became the big-name country act Toby Keith, and he and Wilder are still friends. In 1991, Wilder released tape of original songs that was titled *Twenty Songs, Ten Bucks—Tirk Wilder*. He wrote "The Eyes of the Ranger," 39 seconds of which are the theme song to the CBS TV show *Walker, Texas Ranger*, starring Chuck Norris.

Wilder says, "At this point in life, I am very selective about the gigs I will play, to wit: I will no longer play in the presence of cigarette smoke or liquor consumption. I now play engagements with myself and my guitar only (no more drum machines and synthesizers). I am a singer-songwriter, and since Garth Brooks,

Lionel Richie, or Willie Nelson haven't done any of my songs yet, I'm going follow their example and play only my own stuff."

JONI RICE

Drummer, Music Teacher, and Performing Musician

What do you do, and how long have you been making your living in music?
I play drums in and manage my family's band, teach 45 students privately, teach adjunct at a community college, teach part time at a private school, and direct a church choir. I have been making a living in music for 21 years.

What made you decide to make your living in music?
I grew up in a musical family, started taking piano lessons at age 5 and drum lessons in the fourth grade, and started playing in the band at 13.

Is there a spouse or family member involved with you in your music career? If so, who, and what does he or she do?
My father was the leader and solo trumpet player of a big-band he started in the '30s. He passed away in 1995. My mother joined the band in 1962 playing piano and singing, and my sister and I joined the band in 1976. My sister was 12 and plays the bass.

What has been the highlight of your music career, up to this point?
One night I played percussion for Gladys Knight, and one night I played with the Brazilian percussionist Airto. My family's band has been the guest artist with many symphonies in the Oklahoma/Texas area. We also were named Oklahoma Musicians of the Year for 1985. This award was presented by Governor George Nigh in the capitol building.

What has been the lowest point of your music career, up to this point?
I played with a country band for four months.

Have there been any other opportunities as a direct result of your music career?
My years performing with the family band have allowed us to take memorable trips to many foreign countries and exotic lands. This year we traveled to Africa and will soon take an Alaskan cruise.

If you could begin your music career all over again, what would you do differently?
I would practice more and would go to the right school sooner, a school that would teach me what I wanted to know.

What advice would you like to share with aspiring musicians?
- Be a student of music, get the right teacher, and be versatile. Listen to lots of different kinds of music. I have made my living doing many different things in music and playing many different styles, including everything from sight-reading in a big-band to playing in an orchestra to playing R&B to playing Latin music. Don't ever turn a gig down because you don't think you're capable of doing it.
- Practice hard and don't compare yourself with others. Get as good as *you* can be. Be patient.
- Be dependable and easy to work with. Being a manager for a band, I know I hire people that are proficient at their instruments, always show up on time, and are easy to deal with.

The Rice Dance Band's Bio

The Rice Dance Band Featuring Mr. June Carter
The Rices have been performing together for twenty years. They are the family of Floyd "Red" Rice who started the band over 50 years ago. They were named Oklahoma Musicians of The Year for 1985. They performed Cabaret Pops Concerts with many symphonies in the region and they play many terrific parties.

Lou Ann Rice is a freelance musician who works seven days a week as organist at Casady School and Church of the Savior and pianist everywhere else in town with styles ranging from classical to rock & roll.

Donna is a math teacher at Taft Middle School and has her Master's in math, but her real life is playing bass and singing backup with the band.

Joni, the drummer, has a Master's degree in music, is a freelance musician, teaches privately and at OKC Community College and Casady School, and is choir director at Church of the Savior.

Three years ago they were joined by Mr. June Carter, who adds smooth vocals to every style of music ranging from Nat King Cole to James Brown. He was named 1985 Male Country Vocalist by the Oklahoma Opry.

Together they make the most versatile and fun band in Oklahoma City. They have one recording out and will release two more this fall, a Christmas tape/CD and a solo piano tape/CD. You can contact them for booking or recording information.

They can play all styles of music, whether you want a country/rock band or a jazz band. They also come in all sizes from a solo piano to a 23-piece big-band with strings, and everything in between.

JOE WHITECOTTON

Jazz Trumpet Player, Bandleader of the Joe Whitecotton Trio/Quartet

I started playing professionally when I was 18 (in 1955) in Miami, Florida. I played trumpet in jazz groups (mostly traditional and Dixieland) throughout my college years and was able to play in most of the big hotels and clubs in Miami Beach. It was apparent by 1959, however, that rock was going to take over and there would be little work for trumpet players so I chose a career as an anthropologist. I got a Ph.D. from the University of Illinois and started teaching at Oklahoma University in 1967.

I had stopped playing, but I resumed about 1970. My participation since then has been mainly to earn supplementary income but also for the joy of playing jazz. In fact, in the 1980s I made a trip to Europe with some musicians from here and we played jazz at various places in Austria, Italy, France, and Switzerland. It was obvious that jazz is much more appreciated there than it is here.

My biggest problem is getting people to come to the venues where we play to support the music. I front both a jazz trio and a quartet that plays mainstream jazz ranging from swing to bossa nova to bop, and we usually play at least two nights a week, sometimes more. It's frustrating how little support there really is for America's classic music in America. I've been fortunate that I've had two regular gigs in the last year, one of which lasted for nine months. Both were at restaurants. We received many positive comments on the music from customers but found that there just weren't enough people who were willing to come out on a regular basis to listen. And this is in a college town

Build and Manage Your Music Career

(Norman, Oklahoma) where jazz should be supported. There are only one or two other regular jazz groups in Norman.

In the future I may try to do more with the traditional jazz festival route. I'm told that if you're willing to travel on weekends you'll find many enthusiastic jazz fans out there, particularly in California and Florida. What I will do here is to continue to persist. My group gets smaller and smaller each year to try to accommodate both the low pay scale and demand. I now use a trio or a quartet while I used to have a six-piece group. I'm now considering using MIDI for drums and bass and some doubling of melodic lines.

LYNN BUSH

Jazz Singer

What do you do, and how long have you been making your living in music?
I am a singer, working as a jazz vocalist, fronting my own group of musicians. I have been singing professionally for over 25 years. I started as a backup singer with a rhythm and blues band.

What made you decide to make your living in music?
I had no choice about becoming a singer. I have always sung. It is as natural for me as talking and I have always known I would be a singer. I am still working on making my living as a full-time singer. As a single individual, it is difficult for me to support myself in this style of music without an outside income source. I support my music as a craft by working in the marketing and public relations field. My decision to work toward a fully focused career in music came about when I began to believe that my talents as a jazz performer would be accepted on a global basis and that my work in developing a network for accessing that level of performance venue was beginning to pay off.

Is there a spouse or family member involved with you in your music career? If so, who, and what does he or she do?
I have no spouse. I get much needed moral support and encouragement from my family, who are my biggest fans.

What has been the highlight of your music career, up to this point?
One of my biggest thrills was the day that I broke through my concentration barriers and could focus entirely on the music at the moment it was being made. For the first time, I felt a oneness with the music that really suspended time and space.

Being in the moment, purely one with the song, I could really feel it from my heart with no distractions to interfere with the intent. It was a very honest moment. It was a discipline breakthrough.

Also, I was recently paid the highest compliment when a patron of the club I was playing in told me that I talk exactly the way I sing. Speaking through the music is what I strive to do, and I felt as though I had been successful that evening.

What has been the lowest point of your music career, up to this point?
There are low points all the time. I try not to qualify them by intensity because that can start to overwhelm me. I look at those times as growth periods, whether they be due to bad decisions on my part or circumstances beyond my control. I see how I could have handled the situation better and move on, learning as I go and using the experience as a new perspective on life. Ultimately, life is what we bring to the music. That is what makes it individual and unique to each artist.

Have there been any other opportunities as a direct result of your music career?
Oddly enough, I've learned a lot of different skills in my quest for the music career I have been working toward my entire life—negotiation, marketing, public relations, promotions, production. I've become a fairly savvy businesswoman in the process, but maybe that would have happened anyway.

If you could begin your music career all over again, what would you do differently?
Practice more. But actually I think I have made multiple starts in my career. Each time I work harder and smarter based upon what I have learned on any previous effort to break through to a higher professional level. Each time, I get closer to the level of performance I wish to achieve that will open the door to global opportunities.

What advice would you like to share with aspiring musicians?
- Be honest with yourself, know your strengths and weaknesses.
- Respect all animals including other musicians.
- Know the difference between the music business and music.

Classical Guitarist

What do you do, and how long have you been making your living in music?

I'm a solo classical guitarist and have been performing professionally for over 20 years.

What made you decide to make your living in music?

It's a dream I've had from the beginning inspired by my father who also makes a living at it.

Is there a spouse or family member involved with you in your music career? If so, who, and what does he or she do?

My father, Manuel, is a guitarist and vocalist, and my brother Mark is a guitarist, composer, songwriter, and vocalist. On rare occasions we will get together and play mariachi music and more, but we all do our solo gigs 99% of the time.

What has been the highlight of your music career, up to this point?

Being asked to play in France twice for the Atkins/Dadi Guitar Festival, and also at the Chet Atkins Appreciation Society (CAAS) Festival in Nashville the last three summers. And finally, releasing six solo guitar CDs independently.

What has been the lowest point of your music career, up to this point?

Setting up for concerts where nobody shows up or knows me. Not getting paid for a gig. Having someone cancel on me at the last minute.

Have there been any other opportunities as a direct result of your music career? If so, what?

Writing a column for early issues of Fingerstyle Guitar Magazine, doing television and radio promotions, and opening for larger acts and being asked to play for greater events.

If you could begin your music career all over again, what would you do differently?

Study with a good teacher from the beginning. Being self-taught for seven years has forced me to work on breaking a lot of bad habits to this day. Listen and study all types of guitar players, live or on recordings. I recommend concentrated practice (not just playing around). And practice with a metronome! (I've never had great rhythm.)

What advice would you like to share with aspiring musicians?
- Don't be more than you are.
- Believe in yourself.
- Accumulate as much knowledge about your instrument as possible and execute your abilities with ease.

SAAD

**Q Productions,
Studio Production Director**

What do you do, and how long have you been making your living in music?
I am a production director and work in several clubs as a music director. I also edit music and do remixes. I have been making a living in the music industry for about 10 years.

What made you decide to make your living in music?
I wanted to help musicians and athletic dancers to achieve their goals in life.

Is there a spouse or family member involved with you in your music career? If so, who, and what does he or she do?
My girlfriend/partner/soon-to-be fiancée also works as my business manager.

What has been the highlight of your music career, up to this point?
Starting my own business and not working for anyone else. I don't have to answer to anyone, and I make my own hours.

What has been the lowest point of your music career, up to this point?
Not having enough hours in the day to accomplish everything.

Have there been any other opportunities as a direct result of your music career? If so, what?
I have been able to expand from being known locally to being known nationwide.

If you could begin your music career all over again, what would you do differently?
I would advertise earlier.

What advice would you like to share with aspiring musicians?
- Trust in what you believe in.
- Go with your gut feelings.
- Learn one new thing a day.

Singer

What do you do?
I'm a singer and songwriter.

What made you decide to make your living in music?
I started out as a ballet dancer, and after an injury I began to sing as another way to express myself through an artistic medium.

Is there a spouse or family member involved with you in your music career? If so, who, and what does he or she do?
Not at present. Initially, when I was working in Los Angeles, I had a close relationship with a member of a prominent recording group. He was and still is a tremendous influence on my music.

What has been the highlight of your music career, up to this point?
Being a warm-up act in L.A. for major recording artists. Also, being asked to record original songs for a team of writers that wrote material for Gladys Knight, Dionne Warwick, the Jackson Five, and others.

What has been the lowest point of your music career, up to this point?
The fact that in my previous marriage I was not allowed to practice my art, which left a major void.

Have there been any other opportunities as a direct result of your music career? If so, what?
I'm planning on recording my original compositions.

If you could begin your music career all over again, what would you do differently?
Never stop doing my music.

What advice would you like to share with aspiring musicians?
Years ago, when Kenny Rodgers was at the top of the charts, I had the opportunity to talk with him about how to make it in the music business. He said perseverance was the key, so persevere. When there are dry spells—and there will be—take every opportunity to perform, even of it's for free.

**Keyboardist/Vocalist,
Husband-and-Wife Duo
Affinity**

What do you do?

I am a keyboardist and vocalist currently performing with Affinity, a duo act doing engagements at various clubs and supper clubs in the Oklahoma City area. I also run RP Productions, a preproduction studio specializing in video beds, jingles, video theme songs, artist demos, and original composition. I also do promotional graphic design (computer based) for local Oklahoma City clients out of the same location.

What made you decide to make your living in music?

There were was never any question about my career choice. Music simply came as the most logical and personally rewarding endeavor for me.

Is there a spouse or family member involved with you in your music career? If so, who, and what does he or she do?

My wife, Lynn Koch Powell, performs with me in our duo act. Lynn is without a doubt Oklahoma City's most accomplished jazz/pop vocalist. I'm sure you will agree the first time you hear her perform!

What has been the highlight of your music career, up to this point?

My musical career has had many memorable moments. I have opened the show for dozens of famous recording artists from country to jazz to rock. One that stands out is opening up for Blood, Sweat, and Tears at the Oklahoma City Civic Center— definitely an experience I won't forget. Some of the most enjoyable memories are my early years when I was employed as a sideman for the Coasters. Big fun! Although country is not my musical style of choice, opening for artists like Merle Haggard, Lee Greenwood, Richochet, and Wade Hayes, to name a few, have been learning experiences that would be invaluable to any musician's career.

What has been the lowest point of your music career, up to this point?

I have been blessed with pretty good luck throughout my music endeavors. I've never been unemployed for any mentionable period of time, and I've been fortunate to meet other artists who have been helpful and compassionate enough to share their experiences.

Have there been any other opportunities as a direct result of your music career? If so, what?
Being a keyboardist led directly to computer editing at a hard run. Digital sequencing and digital audio editing pretty much make up today's studio chores. I have been involved in these aspects for some time now and they have led naturally to graphic design, computer-hardware troubleshooting, software installation and design, and other useful tools that I never thought I'd be doing ten years ago.

If you could begin your music career all over again, what would you do differently?
I would be a smarter money manager. I can look back and see that putting profits back into the music business is what makes a self-employed musician grow in his career many times faster than otherwise!

What advice would you like to share with aspiring musicians?
Persevere!!!... don't give up... go do what you love and go where your creativity leads you. Stay away from drugs as well as large recording industry conglomerates!!!

LYNN KOCH POWELL

**Vocalist,
Husband-and-Wife Duo
Affinity**

What do you do, and how long have you been making your living in music?
I have been a professional vocalist since 1974 and also write original music.

What made you decide to make your living in music?
I started singing in church and rock bands in high school and decided I wanted to go professional.

Is there a spouse or family member involved with you in your music career? If so, who, and what does he or she do?
My husband, Robert Powell, is a musician who sequences music, with his main instrument being keyboards. He also sequences various commercial projects. We've been recently performing a variety of music as a duo act in various local dinner clubs, country clubs, and some dance clubs.

What has been the highlight of your music career, up to this point?
I performed at the Las Vegas Hilton in 1982. Then I started performing with my husband in a band back in 1985. The band was called Double Take, and then the name changed to The Truth and then to RPM. We stayed very busy and there wasn't any kind of music our band couldn't conquer. We have also written some original tunes together which I hope one day will make us successful.

Have there been any other opportunities as a direct result of your music career? If so, what?
Yes. I've been cowriting commercials with my husband and also recording vocal tracks for various projects, such as commercials, television theme songs, and other original compositions.

If you could begin your music career all over again, what would you do differently?
I would move to a town that would offer better opportunities before I raised a family.

What advice would you like to share with aspiring musicians?
- Never give up music or you will regret it one day.
- Work hard and keep fresh by learning something new all the time.
- Challenge yourself with things you never thought you would be able to accomplish.

EUKLID HART

Pianist

What do you do, and how long have you been making your living in music?
I work as a pianist but have recently renewed an interest in the trumpet, the instrument I began on. I have worked in big-bands and combos, and as a soloist, for the past 37 years.

What made you decide to make your living in music?
An innate inability to do anything else. Seriously, I decided to be a musician while in high school. As for performance, when I was 18 and a student at Loyola University, the dean of the music school suggested that I audition for a piano bar at the Hilton Inn in New Orleans, At the time, I really knew only three tunes. They were "Tenderly," "Stardust," and "Lullaby of the Leaves." Although nervous, I decided to try anyway. I played the first two tunes I knew, after which the hotel manager asked me if I could

take requests. I stuttered, "Okay, I guess." He then asked me to play his favorite, "Lullaby of the Leaves." I started the gig the following week, played six hours a night for 16 weeks, earned enough money to by a new car and piano, and decided to play for a living. I had a day job once, but it only lasted a week.

Is there a spouse or family member involved with you in your music career? If so, who, and what does he or she do?
No, although my two sons are musicians, and they are presently playing in their own band.

What has been the highlight of your music career, up to this point?
Scoring a J.D. Spradlin movie, *The Only Way Home.*

What has been the lowest point of your music career, up to this point?
Being out of work for a month with a family to support was no fun. I had to take out a bank loan.

Have there been any other opportunities as a direct result of your music career? If so, what?
I've had the opportunity to travel a lot lately, especially to a spa in Mexico where I perform regularly. I enjoy that very much.

If you could begin your music career all over again, what would you do differently?
Having received a Master's degree and completed quite a few hours in a doctoral program, I often think that I would have enjoyed a teaching career.

What advice would you like share with aspiring musicians?
- If you have any doubt at all about your talent, do something else professionally.
- Always try to see in your mind what you hear, and hear what you see.
- Learn as much as you can about the business of music.

MORRIS McCRAVEN

Tenor Sax

What do you do, and how long have you been making your living in music?
I play tenor sax and started performing in 1961.

What made you decide to make your living in music?
I had a musical background and a love for the art.

What has been the highlight of your music career, up to this point?
Recording albums and CDs, attending the 15th annual Grammy Awards 1973, performing with the Ultimate Rhythm and Blues Cruise in 1997 and the King Biscuit Blues Festival, also in 1997.

What has been the lowest point of your music career?
I missed a performance for the first time ever in 1997.

Have there been any other opportunities as a direct result of your music a career?
I played the leading role in a (Black Liberated Arts) play.

If you could begin your music career all over again, what would you do differently?
I'd start sooner, at a younger age.

What would you like to share with aspiring musicians?
Love what you do, and be consistent.

Musical Terms and Music-Related Resources

COMMON MUSICAL TERMS

A piano teacher and performing-musician friend asked one day, "Maurice, why don't you include a list of common musical terms? I get so frustrated working with musicians who don't even know what a rubato is." "A what?" I replied. Here's the list.

accent	Placed over or under a note that gets special emphasis or simply, play the note louder.
accidental	A sharp or flat not given in the key signature.
adagio	Slowly.
allegro	Quickly, happily.
andante	Moving along (at walking speed).
a tempo	Resume original speed.
crescendo	Gradually louder.
da capo (D.C.) al fine	Repeat from the beginning and play to the *fine* (end).
diminuendo	Gradually softer; also *decrescendo*.
dynamics	Changes in how loud or soft you play.
fermata	Indicates that a note should be held longer than its written value.
fine	The end.

first ending	When part of a song is repeated, measures to be played only the first time are indicated under a bracket.
flat	Lowers a note one half step; play the next key to the left on a keyboard, or the next fret toward the nut on a guitar.
forte	Loud.
half step	The distance from one key to the very next one on a keyboard, or from one fret to the next on a guitar (also called a *semitone*).
harmonic interval	Two tones sounded together.
incomplete measure	The measure at the beginning of a piece when it has fewer beats than shown in the time signature. (The missing beats are made up in the last measure.)
interval	The difference in pitch between two tones.
key signature	The number of sharps or flats in a key, written at the beginning of each line of the music.
legato	Smoothly connected. Often indicated by a slur over or under the notes.
major scale	A series of eight notes made of two tetrachords joined by a whole step.
melodic interval	Two tones sounded separately, in succession.
mezzo forte	Moderately loud.
moderato	Moderately fast.
natural sign	Cancels a sharp or flat.
octave sign	When placed over notes, play them one octave higher than written.
piano	Soft.
repeat signs	Repeat from the beginning, or repeat the measures between the double bars.
ritardando (ritard.)	Gradually slower.

rubato	Played without strict timing or meter.
second ending	The measures under the bracket are played the second time only (see *first ending*).
sharp	Raises a note one half step; play the next key to the right on a keyboard, or the next fret toward the bridge on a guitar.
staccato	Short and detached; indicated by a dot over or under the note.
tempo	The speed at which a song is played.
tetrachord	Four notes in alphabetical order, having the pattern of whole step–whole step–half step, e.g., D-E-F#-G.
time signature	Indicated at the beginning of a piece or section of a piece: the top number shows the number of beats in each measure; the bottom number shows the kind of note that gets one beat.
whole step	Two half steps.

State arts councils offer unique programs designed to aid performing artists and to encourage cities to explore their state's growing pool of musicians and performing artists.

Alabama State Council on the Arts & the Alabama Artists Gallery
201 Monroe Street
Montgomery, AL 36130-1800
Phone: (334) 242-4076/Fax: (334) 240-3269
Email: staff@arts.state.al.us
Web site: www.arts.state.al.us

Alaska State Council on the Arts
411 West 4th Avenue, Suite 1E
Anchorage, AK 99501-2343
Phone: (907) 269-6610/Toll-free: (888) 278-7424
Fax: (907) 269-6601
E-Mail: info@aksca.org
Web site: www.aksca.org

Arizona Commission on the Arts
417 W. Roosevelt
Phoenix, AZ 85003-1326
Phone: (602) 255-5882/Fax: (602) 256-0282
Email: general@ArizonaArts.org
Website: az.arts.asu.edu/artscomm

Arkansas Arts Council
1500 Tower Building, 323 Center Street
Little Rock, AR 72201
Phone: (501) 324-9766/Fax: (501) 324-9207
TTD: (501) 324-9150
Email: info@arkansasarts.com
Website: www.arkansasarts.com

California Arts Council
1300 I Street, Suite 930
Sacramento, CA 95814
Phone: (916) 322-6555
e-mail cac@cwo.com
Website: www.cac.ca.gov

Colorado Council on the Arts
750 Pennsylvania St.
Denver, CO 80203
Phone: (303) 894-2617
Email: coloarts@state.co.us
Website: www.coloarts.state.co.us.

Connecticut Commission on the Arts
One Financial Plaza
755 Main St.
Hartford, CT 06103
Phone: (860) 566-4770/Fax: (860) 566-6462
Email: kdemeo@ctarts.org
Website: www.ctarts.org

Delaware Division of the Arts/Delaware State Arts Council
Carvel State Office Building
820 North French Street
Wilmington, Delaware 19801
Phone: (302) 577-8278 (from New Castle County)
(302) 739-5304 (from Kent or Sussex Counties)
Fax: (302) 577-6561
Email: delarts@artswire.org
Website: http://www.artsdel.org

DC Commission on the Arts & Humanities
An Agency of the Government of the District of Columbia
410 8th Street, NW, 5th Floor
Washington, DC 20004
Phone: (202) 724-5613/Fax: (202) 727-4135
Email: carrien@tmn.com
Website: www.capaccess.org/dccah

Division of Cultural Affairs
Florida Department of State
The Capitol
Tallahassee, FL 32399-0250
Phone: (850) 487-2980/Fax: (850) 922-5259
Email: wmoss@mail.dos.state.fl.us
Website: www.dos.state.fl.us/dca

Georgia Council for the Arts
260 14th St. NW, Suite 401
Atlanta, GA 30318
Phone: (404) 685-2787/Fax: (404) 685-2788
TTD: (404) 685-2799
E-Mail: info@arts-ga.com
Website: www.state.ga.us/georgia-arts

The Hawaii State Foundation on Culture and the Arts
44 Merchant Street
Honolulu, HI 96813
Phone: (808) 586-0300/Fax: (808) 586-0308
TDD: (808) 586-0740
Email: sfca@sfca.state.hi.us
Website: www.state.hi.us/sfca

Idaho Commission on the Arts
P.O. Box 83720
Boise, ID 83720-0008
Phone: (208) 334-2119/Toll-free: (800) 278-3863
Fax: (208) 334-2488
Email: bgarrett@ica.state.id.us
Website: www2.state.id.us/arts

Illinois Arts Council
James R. Thompson Center, 100 West Randolph, Suite 10-500
Chicago, IL 60601
Phone: (312) 814-6750/Toll-free: (800) 237-6994
TTY: (312) 814-4831/Fax: (312) 814-1471
Email: info@arts.state.il.us
Website: www.state.il.us/agency/iac

Indiana Arts Commission
402 West Washington Street, Room 72
Indianapolis, IN 46204
Phone: (317) 232-1268/Fax: (317) 232-5595
Website: www.aaae.org/councils/indiana.html

Iowa Arts Council
600 E. Locust
Des Moines, IA 50319-0290
Phone: (515) 281-4451/Fax: (515) 242-6498
TDD: (515) 242-5147
Email: Bruce.Williams@dca.state.ia.us
Website: www.culturalaffairs.org/iac/index.html

Kansas Arts Commission
700 SW Jackson, Suite 1004
Topeka, KS 66603-3761
Phone: (785) 296-3335/Fax: (785) 296-4989
Email: KAC@arts.state.ks.us
Website: arts.state.ks.us

Kentucky Arts Council
Old Capitol Annex, 300 West Broadway
Frankfort, KY 40601
Phone: (502) 564-3757/Toll-free: (888) 833-2787
Email: kyarts@mail.state.ky.us
Website: www.kyarts.org

Louisiana Division of the Arts
P.O. Box 44247
Baton Rouge, LA 70804-4247
Phone: (225) 342-8180/Fax: (225) 342-8173
Email: arts@crt.state.la.us
Website: www.crt.state.la.us/arts

The Maine Arts Commission
55 Capitol Street
25 State House Station
Augusta, ME 04333-0025
Phone: (207) 287-2724/Fax: (207) 287-2335
TTY: (207) 287-2360
Email: jan.poulin@state.me.us
Website: www.mainearts.com

Maryland State Arts Council (MSAC)
175 West Ostend Street, Suite E,
Baltimore, MD 21230
Phone: (410) 767-6555/TDD (410) 333-4519
Fax: (410) 333-1062
Email: tcolvin@mdbusiness.state.md.us
Website: www.msac.org

Massachusetts Cultural Council
10 St. James Avenue, 3rd Floor
Boston, MA 02116-3803
Phone: (617) 727-3668/Toll-free: (800) 232-0960 (in MA only)
Fax: (617) 727-0044
TTY: (617) 338-9153
Email: web@art.state.ma.us
Website: www.massculturalcouncil.org

The Michigan Council for Arts and Cultural Affairs
525 West Ottawa
P.O. Box 30705
Lansing, MI 48909
Phone: (517) 241-3970
Website: www.commerce.state.mi.us/arts/home.htm

Minnesota State Arts Board
Park Square Court
400 Sibley St., Suite 200
St. Paul, MN 55101-1928
Phone: (651) 215-1600/Toll-free: (800) 866-2787
TTY: (651) 215-6235/Fax: (651) 215-1602
Email: msab@state.mn.us
Website: www.arts.state.mn.us

Mississippi Arts Commission
239 North Lamar Street, Suite 207
Jackson, MS 39201
Phone: (601) 359-6030/Fax: (601) 359-6008
Website: www.arts.state.ms.us

Missouri Arts Council
Wainwright State Office Complex
111 N. 7th St., Suite 105
St. Louis, MO 63101-2188
Phone: (314) 340-6845/Fax: (314) 340-7215
TDD: (800) 735-2966
Email: moarts@mail.state.mo.us
Website: www.missouriartscouncil.org

Montana Arts Council
P.O. Box 202201
Helena MT. 59620-2201
Phone : (406) 444-6430/Fax: (406)444-6548
Email: mac@state.mt.us
Website: www.art.state.mt.us

Nebraska Arts Council
Joslyn Carriage House
3838 Davenport Street
Omaha, Nebraska 68131-2329
Phone: (402) 595-2122/Toll free: (800) 341-4067
TDD: (402) 595-2122
FAX: (402) 595-2334
Email: cmalloy@nebraskaartscouncil.org
Website: www.nebraskaartscouncil.org

Nevada Arts Council
716 North Carson St., Suite A
Carson City, NV 89701
Phone: (775) 687-6680
Website: dmla.clan.lib.nv.us/docs/arts

New Hampshire State Council on the Arts
40 N. Main St.
Concord, NH 03301-4974
Phone: (603) 271-2789/TTY/TDD: (800) 735-2964
Fax: (603) 271-3584
Email: mdurkee@nharts.state.nh.us
Website: www.state.nh.us/nharts

New Jersey State Council on the Arts
P.O. Box 306, 225 West State Street
Trenton, NJ 08625
Phone: (609) 292-6130/TDD: (609) 633-1186
Fax: (609) 989-1440
Email: njsca@arts.sos.state.nj.us
Website: www.njartscouncil.org

New Mexico Arts, A Division of the Office of Cultural Affairs
P.O.Box 1450
Santa Fe, NM 87504-1450
Phone: (505) 827-6490/Toll-free: (800) 879-4278
Fax: (505) 827-6043
Website: www.nmarts.org

New York State Council on the Arts
915 Broadway, 8th Floor
New York, NY 10010
Phone: (212) 387-7000/TDD: (800) 895-9838.
Email: pinfo@nysca.org
Website: www.nysca.org

North Carolina Arts Council
Department of Cultural Resources
Raleigh, NC 27699-4632
Phone: (919) 733-2111
Email: ardath.weaver@ncmail.net
Website: www.ncarts.org/home.html

North Dakota Council on the Arts
418 E. Broadway, Suite 70
Bismarck, ND 58501-4086
Phone: (701) 328-3954/Fax: (701) 328-3963/TDD: (800) 366-6888
Email: comserv@state.nd.us
Website: www.state.nd.us/arts

Ohio Arts Council
727 E. Main Street
Columbus OH 43205-1796
Phone: (614) 466-2613/Fax: (614) 466-4494
TTY/TDD (800) 750-0750
Email: kcary@oac.state.oh.us
Website: www.oac.state.oh.us/home.html

Okahoma Arts Council
2101 North Lincoln Blvd., Jim Thorpe Building, Suite 640
P.O. Box 52001-2001
Oklahoma City, OK 73152-2001
Phone: (405) 521-2931/Fax: (405) 521-6418
Email: okarts@arts.state.ok.us
Website: www.state.ok.us/~arts

Oregon Arts Commission
775 Summer Street NE, Suite 350
Salem, Oregon 97301-1284
Phone: (503) 986-0082/Toll-free: (800) 233-3306 (in Oregon)
Email: oregon.artscomm@state.or.us
Website: art.econ.state.or.us

Pennsylvania Council on the Arts
Room 216, Finance Building
Harrisburg, PA 17120
Phone: (717) 787-6883/Fax: (717) 783-2538
Web site: www.artsnet.org/pca/pca.html

Rhode Island State Council on the Arts
83 Park Street, 6th Floor
Providence, RI 02903
Phone: (401) 222-3880/Fax: 401) 222-3018
Email: info@risca.state.ri.us
Website: www.risca.state.ri.us

The South Carolina Arts Commission
1800 Gervais St.
Columbia, SC 29201
Phone: (803) 734-8696/Fax: (803) 734-8526/TDD: (803) 734-8983
Email: mayken@arts.state.sc.us
Website: www.state.sc.us/arts

South Dakota Arts Council
800 Governors Dr.
Pierre, SD 57501-2294
Phone: (605) 773-3131/Toll-free: (800) 423-6665
Fax: (605) 773-6962
EMail: sdac@stlib.state.sd.us
Website: www.state.sd.us/deca/sdarts

Tennessee Arts Commission
401 Charlotte Avenue
Nashville, TN 37243-0780
Phone: (615) 741-1701
Email: dadkins@mail.state.tn.us
Website: www.arts.state.tn.us

Texas Commission on the Arts
E. O. Thompson Office Building
920 Colorado, Suite 501
Austin, Texas 78701
Phone: (512) 463-5535/Toll Free: (800) 252-9415
TTY: (512) 475-3327/Fax: (512) 475-2699
Email: front.desk@arts.state.tx.us
Website: www.arts.state.tx.us

The Utah Arts Council
617 E. South Temple
Salt Lake City, UT 84102-1177
Phone: (801) 236-7555/TDD: (800) 346-4128/Fax: (801) 236-7556
Email: tbuhler@arts.state.ut.us
Website: www.dced.state.ut.us/arts

Vermont Arts Council
136 State St., Drawer 33
Montpelier, VT 05633-6001
Phone: (802) 828-3291/TTY: (800) 253-0191/Fax: (802) 828-3363
Email info@arts.vca.state.vt.us
Website: www.vermontartscouncil.org

Virginia Commission for the Arts
Lewis House, 2nd Floor , 223 Governor St.
Richmond, VA 23219-2010
Phone/TDD: (804) 225-3132/Fax: (804) 225-4327
Email: vacomm@artswire.org.
Website: www.artswire.org/~vacomm

Washington State Arts Commission
234 E 8th Avenue, P O Box 42675
Olympia WA 98504-2675
Phone: (360) 753-3860/Fax: (360) 586-5351
Email: pamm@arts.wa.gov
Website: www.wa.gov/art/index.html

The West Virginia Commission on the Arts
WV Division of Culture and History
1900 Kanawha Blvd. E.
Charleston, WV 25305-0300
Phone: (304) 558-0220
Website: www.wvculture.org/arts

Wisconsin Arts Board
101 E. Wilson St., 1st Floor
Madison, WI 53702
Phone: (608) 266-0190
Email: artsboard@arts.state.wi.us
Website: arts.state.wi.us/static

Wyoming Arts Council
2320 Capitol Avenue
Cheyenne, WY 82002
Phone: (307) 777-7742/Fax: (307) 777-5499
Website: commerce.state.wy.us/CR/Arts

OTHER MUSIC-RELATED ORGANIZATIONS

American Academy of Teachers of Singing (AATS)
c/o William Gephart
75 Bank St.
New York, NY 10014
Phone: (212) 242-1836
Website: www.voiceteachersacademy.org

The American Disc Jockey Association
10882 Demarr Road
White Plains, MD 20695
Phone (301) 705-5150/(301) 843-7284
Email: adjanatloffice@adja.org
Website: www.adja.org

American Federation of Musicians (AFM)
1501 Broadway, Suite 600
New York, NY 10036
Phone: (212) 869-1330/Fax: (212) 764-6134
Website: www.afm.org

American Guild of Musical Artists (AGMA)
1727 Broadway
New York, NY 10019
Phone: (212) 265-3687/Fax: (212) 262-9088
Email: AGMA@AGMANatl.com
Website: www.agmanatl.com

American Guild of Variety Artists (AGVA)
184 5th Ave, 6th Floor
New York, NY 10010
Phone: (212) 675-1003/Fax: (212) 633-0097
Email: agvany@aol.com
Website: home.earthlink.net/~agvala/agva1.html

American Institute of Musical Studies
6621 Snider Plaza
Dallas TX 75205
Phone: (214) 363-2683/Fax: (214) 363-6474
aims@airmail.net
Website: www.aimsgraz.org

American Society of Music Copyists
P.O. Box 2557, Times Square Station
New York, NY 10108
Email: ASMC802@aol.com
Website: members.aol.com/asmc802/home.htm

Association for Technology in Music Instruction (ATMI)
c/o Peter R. Webster
School of Music, Northwestern University
Evanston, IL 60208
Phone: (847) 491-5740
Email: pwebster@nwu.edu

Church Music Publishers Association (CMPA)
P.O. Box 158992
Nashville, TN 37215
Phone: (615) 791-0273

Electronic Music Consortium (EMC)
c/o Dr. Thomas Wells
School of Music
Ohio State University
Columbus, OH 43210
Phone: (614) 292-1102

Independent Music Association (IMA)
317 Skyline Lake Dr.
Ringwood, NJ 07456
Phone: (201) 831-1317

Institute for Studies in American Music
Brooklyn College of the City University of New York
2900 Bedford Ave.
Brooklyn, NY 11210-2889
Phone: (718) 951-5655/Fax: (718) 951-4858
Email: isam@brooklyn.cuny.edu
Website: depthome.brooklyn.cuny.edu/isam

International Alliance for Women in Music
(IAWM) Adminitrative Office
Department of Music
422 S. 11th St., Room 209
Indiana University of Pennsylvania
Indiana, PA 15705-1070
Phone: (724) 357-7918/Fax: (724) 357-9570
Email: info@grove.iup.edu
Website: 150.252.8.92/www/iawm

International Association of Jazz Educators (IAJE)
2803 Claflin Road, P.O. Box 724
Manhattan, KS 66505
Phone: (785) 776-8744/Fax: (785) 776-6190
Email: Info@iaje.org
Website: www.iaje.org

International Computer Music Association (ICMA)
2040 Polk St., Suite 330
San Francisco, CA 94109
Phone: (734) 878-3310/Fax: (734) 878-3031
Email: icma@umich.edu
Website: www.computermusic.org

Karaoke International Sing-Along Association (KISA)
2321-B Tapo St., Suite #114
Simi Valley, CA 93063-3023
Phone: (805) 526-5442

MENC: The National Association for Music Education
1806 Robert Fulton Drive
Reston, VA 20191
Phone: (703) 860-4000/Toll-free: (800) 336-3768
Fax: (703) 860-1531
Email: elizabet@menc.org
Website: www.menc.org

Music Educators National Conference (MENC)
MIDI Manufacturers Association (MMA), P.O. Box 3173
La Habra, CA 90632-3173
Fax: (714) 736-9775
Email: mma@midi.org
Website: www.midi.org

Music Publishers' Association
PMB 246, 1562 First Ave.
New York, NY 10028
Phone: (212) 327-4044
mpa-admin@mpa.org
Website: www.mpa.org

Music Teachers National Association (MTNA)
The Carew Tower, 441 Vine St, Suite 505
Cincinnati, OH 45202
Phone: (513) 421-1420
Email: mtnanet@mtna.org
Website: www.mtna.org

National Association of Music Merchants (NAMM)
5790 Armada Drive
Carlsbad, California 92008
Phone: (760) 438-8001
Toll-free (800) 767-6266/Fax: (760) 438-7327
Email: info@namm.com
Website: www.namm.com

The National Association of Pastoral Musicians (NPM)
225 Sheridan St. NW
Washington, DC 20011-1492
Phone: (202) 723-5800/Fax: (202) 723-2262
E-mail:npmsing@npm.org
Website: www.npm.org

The National Association of Teachers of Singing (NATS)
6406 Merrill Rd., Suite B
Jacksonville, FL 32277
Phone: (904) 744-9022/Fax: (904) 744-9033
Email: info@nats.org
Website: www.nats.org

National Guild of Piano Teachers (NGPT)
808 Rio Grande St.
Austin, TX 78701
Phone: (512) 478-5775/Fax: (512) 478-5843
Email: ngpt@aol.com
Website: www.pianoguild.com

National Music Publishers' Association
711 Third Avenue
New York, NY 10017
Phone: (212) 370-5330/Fax: (212) 953-2384
Email: clientservice@harryfox.com
Website: www.nmpa.org

Suzuki Association of America (SAA)
PO Box 17310
Boulder, CO 80308
Phone: (303) 444-0948/Fax: (303) 444-0984
Email: hippo103@hotmail.com
Website: www.suzukiassociation.org

MUSIC-RELATED PUBLICATIONS

Bass Player
Music Player Network, 2800 Campus Drive
San Mateo, CA 94403
Phone: (650) 513-4400/Fax: (650) 513-4642
Email: bassplayer@musicplayer.com
Website: www.bassplayer.com

The Beat
Bongo Productions, PO Box 65856
Los Angeles, CA 90065
Phone: (323) 257-2328/Fax: (323) 257-2461
Email: getthebeat@aol.com

Billboard
BPI Communications, Inc., 770 Broadway
New York, NY 10003
Phone: (646) 654-4696/Fax: (646) 654-4798
Website: www.billboard.com

Bluegrass Unlimited
P.O. Box 111
Broad Run, VA, 20137 USA
Phone: (540) 349-8181
Email: info@bluegrassmusic.com
Website: www.bluegrassmusic.com

Circus Magazine
3 W. 18th St.
New York, NY 10011
Website: www.circusmagazine.com

Down Beat
102 N. Haven Rd.
Elmhurst, IL, 60126 USA
Phone:(630) 941-2030
Email: editor@downbeat.com
Website: www.downbeat.com

Electronic Musician
Intertec Publishing
6400 Hollis St., Suite 12
Emeryville, CA 94608
Phone: 510-653-3307/Fax: 510-653-5142
Website: www.emusician.com

EQ
United Entertainment Media
460 Park Ave. S., 9th Floor
New York, NY 10016
Phone: 212-378-0400/Fax: 212-378-2160
Email: eqmagazine@aol.com
Website: www.eqmag.com

Guitar Player
Music Player Network,
2800 Campus Drive
San Mateo, CA 94403
Phone: (650) 513-4300/Fax: (650) 513-4646
Email: guitplyr@musicplayer.com
Website: www.guitarplayer.com

Jazz Educators Journal
P.O. Box 724
Manhattan, KS, 66505 USA
Phone: (785) 776-8744/Fax: (785) 776-6190
Email: Info@iaje.org
Website: wwwiaje.org

JazzTimes
8737 Colesville Rd., 5th Floor
Silver Spring, MD, 20910-3921
Phone: (800) 866-7664/Fax: (301) 588-5531
Website: www.jazztimes.com

Living Blues
301 Hill Hall
University, MS, 38677 USA
Phone: (622) 915-5742/Fax: (622) 915-7842
Email: lblues@olemiss.edu
Web: www.livingbluesonline.com

Keyboard
Music Player Network
2800 Campus Drive
San Mateo, CA 94403
Phone: (650) 513-4300/Fax: (650) 513-4661
Email: keyboard@musicplayer.com
Website: www.keyboardonline.com

Melody Maker
IPC Magazines Ltd.
Kings Reach Tower, 26th Floor, Stamford St.
London, SE1 9LS
Phone: (44) 207-2617584/Fax: (44) 207-2615504
Web: www.ipc.co.uk/pubs/melomake.htm

MIX
Intertec Publishing
6400 Hollis St., Suite 12
Emeryville, CA 94608
Phone: 510-653-3307/Fax: 510-653-5142
Website: www.mixonline.com

Music News
Texas Music News
1506 Pearl
League City, TX 77573
Phone: (281) 480-6397/Fax: (281) 332-7540
Email: musicnew@neosoft.com
Website: www.neosoft.com/~musicnew

Onstage
Intertec Publishing
6400 Hollis St., Suite 12
Emeryville, CA 94608
Phone: 510-653-3307/Fax: 510-653-5142

Relix Magazine
180 Varick St., 5th Floor
New York, NY 10014
Phone: (646) 230-0100/Fax: (646) 230-0200
Email: editor@relix.com
Website: www.relix.com

Remix
Intertec Publishing
6400 Hollis St., Suite 12
Emeryville, CA 94608
Phone: 510-653-3307/Fax: 510-653-5142

Rolling Stone
Wenner Media, Inc.
1290 Avenue of the Americas, 2nd Floor
New York, NY 10104
Phone: (212) 484-1616/Fax: (212) 767-8205
Web: www.rollingstone.com

Tape Op
PO Box 507
Sacramento, CA 95812
Phone: (916) 444-8200/Fax: 916-444-8972
Email: info@tapeop.com
Web: www.tapeop.com

Epilogue

After the breakup of my band After Five Jazz in 1993, it took me a while to get back into the groove. But once I got started, it was a breeze. I wholeheartedly welcomed new ideas that brought the promise of new beginnings, while silently abating my apprehension and fear of failure.

You're sharp enough to know that your band's business affairs—booking gigs, bookkeeping, and general management—should be in competent hands and, fortunately for you, those hands are likely to be your own. It is up to you how your own scenario will unfold. Use your time wisely and take advantage of every resource available to you. As you nurture all of your collective efforts, talents, and skills, embrace the thought of gaining first-hand knowledge and the experience of bootstrapping your own music career. *Good luck!*

—*Maurice Johnson*

If you would like to contact the author, write to:
Maurice Johnson
P.O. Box 770083
Orlando, Florida 32877
or e-mail: maurice@giglogic.com

Idleness is the holiday for fools. I said this earlier, and now I want to emphasize it. If you, as an independent working musician/performing artist, are not as busy as you want to be, it is very important that you set some goals. Make yourself a list of important things that must be done in the upcoming months. Don't just conjure up unrealistic goals that are impossible to meet within a 30-day period. Think practically when listing your objectives so you can move closer to your ultimate goal of success.

A practical goal can be as simple as designing a business card for your band. Regardless of what your goals are, get into the habit of writing them down and following through with them in a reasonable amount of time. Refer to the previous chapters' advice and use the following pages to list monthly goals and objectives.

Ten Important *Goals for This Month!* _____

1. _____
2. _____
3. _____
4. _____
5. _____
6. _____
7. _____
8. _____
9. _____
10. _____

Notes _____

_____

_____

_____

_____

_____

_____

_____

_____

_____

_____

_____

_____

Ten **Important** *Goals for This Month!* _____

1. _____
2. _____
3. _____
4. _____
5. _____
6. _____
7. _____
8. _____
9. _____
10. _____

Notes_____

_____

_____

_____

_____

_____

_____

_____

_____

_____

_____

_____

Ten **Important** *Goals for This Month!* _____

1. _____
2. _____
3. _____
4. _____
5. _____
6. _____
7. _____
8. _____
9. _____
10. _____

Notes_____

_____

_____

_____

_____

_____

_____

_____

_____

_____

_____

_____

Ten **Important** *Goals for This Month!* _____

1._____
2._____
3._____
4._____
5._____
6._____
7._____
8._____
9._____
10._____

Notes_____

_____
_____
_____
_____
_____
_____
_____
_____
_____
_____
_____
_____

Ten **Important** *Goals for This Month!* _____

1. _____
2. _____
3. _____
4. _____
5. _____
6. _____
7. _____
8. _____
9. _____
10. _____

Notes _____

_____

_____

_____

_____

_____

_____

_____

_____

_____

_____

_____

Ten **Important** *Goals for This Month!* _____

1. _____
2. _____
3. _____
4. _____
5. _____
6. _____
7. _____
8. _____
9. _____
10. _____

Notes _____

_____
_____
_____
_____
_____
_____
_____
_____
_____
_____
_____

Ten **Important** *Goals for This Month!* _____

1. _____
2. _____
3. _____
4. _____
5. _____
6. _____
7. _____
8. _____
9. _____
10. _____

Notes _____

_____

_____

_____

_____

_____

_____

_____

_____

_____

_____

_____

_____

Ten **Important** *Goals for This Month!* _____

1._____
2._____
3._____
4._____
5._____
6._____
7._____
8._____
9._____
10._____

Notes_____

_____
_____
_____
_____
_____
_____
_____
_____
_____
_____
_____
_____
_____

Ten **Important** *Goals for This Month!* _____

1. _____
2. _____
3. _____
4. _____
5. _____
6. _____
7. _____
8. _____
9. _____
10. _____

Notes _____

_____
_____
_____
_____
_____
_____
_____
_____
_____
_____
_____
_____

Ten **Important** *Goals for This Month!* _____

1._____

2._____

3._____

4._____

5._____

6._____

7._____

8._____

9._____

10._____

Notes_____

_____

_____

_____

_____

_____

_____

_____

_____

_____

_____

_____

Ten **Important** *Goals for This Month!* _____

1. _____
2. _____
3. _____
4. _____
5. _____
6. _____
7. _____
8. _____
9. _____
10. _____

Notes_____

_____
_____
_____
_____
_____
_____
_____
_____
_____
_____
_____

Ten **Important** *Goals for This Month!* _____

1._____

2._____

3._____

4._____

5._____

6._____

7._____

8._____

9._____

10._____

Notes_____

_____

_____

_____

_____

_____

_____

_____

_____

_____

_____

_____

Suggested Reading

The New! Working Musician's One Year Organizer, by Maurice Johnson.
Mel Bay Publishing, 1996.

The Independent Working Musician, by Mary Cosola.
Mix Books, 1998.

How To Out-Negotiate Anyone, by Leo Reilly.
Bob Adams Publishing.